Jesus is Alive!

by Dale Armstrong

A publication of the Armada Network

Copyright © 2023 by Dale Armstrong

First Edition

Lancaster, Pennsylvania

All rights reserved. No part of this book may be used or reproduced in any manner whatsoever without written permission of the copyright owner, except in the case of brief quotations embodied in articles and reviews.

For information write director@armadanetwork.org

For Teri,
who reveals more
of Jesus than anyone
I've ever known.

Table of Contents

Only Believe 13
The Power of Jesus Christ 23
Jesus Healed them All..31
The Question Everyone Asks 37
If You Can Believe 47
Miraculous Love 61
The Priority of the Word 71
God's Word is Medicine.......................................77
Learning to Live Free...91
Presumption is not Faith 107
Established in Righteousness 123
Enemies of Faith..131
The Good News 139
The Fellowship of Faith 151
The Origin of Sickness and Disease 165
The God of All Comfort 183
Hear and Be Healed 195

A Word to the Reader

For more than forty years people have come to me for prayer, and I typically ask them, "What would you like from the Lord?" I ask you the same question now, or perhaps you should ask it of yourself. What would you have from the Lord? What do you need from God?

There must be some hunger or thirst in you. What brought you to this book? Do you need healing? Do you have questions about God's will? Do you want to help others who are suffering? Do you want to pray for the sick?

Together we can seek the truth concerning God's will and God's way for the healing of our bodies, for it is the knowledge of the truth that sets us free.[1] There are many who do not know the truth because they have not been told. God's "people perish for lack of knowledge."[2]

In our generation people are amazed when they witness a miracle. Jesus was amazed when He saw their unbelief! Many do not recognize God's presence or understand His healing power. They do not live in the reality that Jesus is alive and actually present, here and now, to heal.

Throughout this book many of the same principles will

---

[1] John 8:32
[2] Hosea 8:6

be repeated from different angles and highlighted by different circumstances. I believe that repetition is the mother of study and sometimes a truth that eludes us one time will become apparent when seen in a different setting. Many truths grow in understanding and application as we consider them over and over. One plants and another waters.

To be clear, I've written this book for you to personally receive your healing, to train believers to pray for the sick, and to answer several questions and objections people generally have concerning divine healing.

Here you will find Biblical truth to build your faith and receive healing from the Lord. Immerse yourself in these chapters, and study them closely. As Lester Sumrall often said, "Feed your faith, and starve your doubts to death!"

Often, it is necessary that we tear down strongholds[1] that have been falsely erected in our minds, before we can receive the truth that sets us free.

I know this is not a short book. It should perhaps have been much longer. At any rate, I believe the effort you give to reading and study will be well worth your time.

It's my prayer, after you have read through these pages, that you understand how the very real and desperate need of healing for the body illuminates the more real and prevailing truth that Jesus Christ is alive, present with us, and doing wonders.

Your personal need, your hunger and your thirst, your

---

[1] 2 Corinthians 10:4,5

sickness and disease, can only be met by the living, resurrected Lord. Let it be as Peter declared, "Jesus Christ heals you!"[1]

Dale Armstrong,
Lancaster, Pennsylvania

---

[1] Acts 9:34

1

Only Believe

We flew through a typhoon to Manila, Philippines, and then on by small plane to the island of Palawan. We crossed mud slides and thick jungle on an overcrowded bus to reach the western shore. Sailing a day further south, we survived twelve foot swells on the Pacific in small boats that didn't belong on water. Heading inland, we waded rivers filled with water buffalo to emerge draping with leeches. We hiked higher into the mountains and deeper into the jungle to meet an unreached tribe, ate roasted Javelina impaled by a spear, and listened to the story of the hunt in wonder and amazement; but none of that compared to the day I saw a half naked man stagger out of the jungle carrying his dying wife in his arms.

We were at the edge of a clearing when he appeared, and immediately people ran towards him, shouting for everyone's attention, shouting for help, shouting for all to come near. They surrounded the staggering man, and many hands lowered his burden to the ground.

My friend, who had invited me to the island of Palawan, called for me to come closer. I ran to join the small group. They were chattering to one another in the Tagalog language. I had no idea what they were saying.

"He carried his wife three days through the jungle," Andrew translated. "She's dying from malaria!" And then in shock and disbelief, he said it again: "He carried his wife three days looking for a doctor to save her."

An old woman felt her pulse, and then stroked the wet and matted hair away from her eyes. She spoke gravely to those standing near, and her tone seemed to be delivering a sentence of death.

The man sat on the ground with his head in his hands. He was exhausted, still breathing heavily, his body bathed in sweat. His wife remained unconscious and unresponsive.

"There's no doctor or medicine here," Andrew said. "If we hire a jeep to carry her out it will take at least five hours to reach a doctor. I don't think she will make it. This woman thinks she'll be dead very soon. They deal with this too often."

We gently pushed our way through the group and knelt beside them. Andrew spoke to the husband and began to share Jesus with him while I laid my hands on the woman's head and commanded death to leave. The Spirit of God rose up in me and with a great sense of authority I spoke life into her body. The healing power of Jesus Christ was imparted to her.

While Andrew was praying the prayer of salvation with

the husband, at that very moment — his wife opened her eyes and looked into mine. I'll never forget those eyes.

The people surrounding us began to shout. Tears streamed down the husband's face. He began to softly clap his calloused, darkened hands. Joy was shining from his face. We were in the presence of two great miracles. God had healed the woman, and saved the man.

He began speaking to his wife, embracing her and kissing her brow. She took a few sips of water. We watched her strength return miraculously. In a few moments she also prayed the prayer of salvation.[1] Our little group had grown larger, many shouting praises to God, and more began to gather.

Andrew said, "I don't believe it." I looked at him and said nothing.

In another moment she was standing, clinging to her husband. A man drove his jeep up to us, and we were encouraged to take her into the city where a doctor could examine her. We joined them on a five hour ride across the remote island.

During the journey, my friend kept looking back over his shoulder at the couple. The husband sat affectionately holding his wife's hand while they were talking back and forth. She was growing stronger and stronger every moment.

For the second time Andrew looked at me and said, "I

---

[1] If you have never prayed the prayer of salvation to declare Jesus Christ the Lord of your life, please turn to the end of this book and read "What Must I do to be Saved? We encourage you to receive Jesus into your heart. You will never be the same again!

don't believe it."

I took a deep breath and said, "I believe it," and then a little more forcefully I said, "Someone has to believe it."

Riding through the jungle that day, my mind was filled with several simple verses from the ministry of Jesus:

Luke 8:41-42; 49-56
41 And, behold, there came a man named Jairus, and he was a ruler of the synagogue: and he fell down at Jesus' feet, and besought him that he would come into his house:
42 For he had one only daughter, about twelve years of age, and she lay a dying…
49 While he yet spake, there cometh one from the ruler of the synagogue's house, saying to him, Thy daughter is dead; trouble not the Master.
50 But when Jesus heard it, he answered him, saying, Fear not: believe only, and she shall be made whole.
51 And when he came into the house, he suffered no man to go in, save Peter, and James, and John, and the father and the mother of the maiden.
52 And all wept, and bewailed her: but he said, Weep not; she is not dead, but sleepeth.
53 And they laughed him to scorn, knowing that she was dead.
54 And he put them all out, and took her by the hand, and called, saying, Maid, arise.
55 And her spirit came again, and she arose straightway: and he commanded to give her meat.

How simple His instructions, but how profound they affect our lives. We should take this to heart.

Jesus said, "*Only believe.*"

Many think that when they pray, God is making a decision. They ask and He decides. As a result, they cannot exercise a sure confidence that they will be healed every time. They have postponed their confidence. They wait as though their prayer for healing is being taken under consideration.

God has made His will clearly known and we should not forget His benefits, "who forgives all our sins, and heals each and everyone of our diseases," (Psalms 103:2,3).

Why pray "Lord, if it be thy will" when He has already made His will known? His decision has already been made. He wants to heal you now.

If God has healed even one person, then the same provision must be made available to all for "He is not a respecter of persons," (Acts 10:34). In his great sermon, Peter declared that Jesus "healed all who were oppressed of the devil" (verse 38). This is absolute: all were healed, and those healed were all oppressed of the devil.

If no one in Peter's day was denied healing, and all those sick were in fact oppressed of the devil — we can be sure of the same today, for "Jesus Christ is the same, yesterday, today and forever," (Hebrews 13:7). The immutable character of God is our assurance.

By healing everyone, Jesus fulfilled the Scriptural promise made by Isaiah (53:4,5) and confirmed by Matthew:

Matthew 8:16,17
16 When the even was come, they brought unto him many that were possessed with devils: and he cast out the spirits with his word, and healed all that were sick:
17 That it might be fulfilled which was spoken by Esaias the prophet, saying, Himself took our infirmities, and bare our sicknesses.

If God were to withhold the provision of healing from anyone then Isaiah's promise would be null and void. If the offer was good then, it is good now. The same provision made for sin was made for healing, and if the offer of healing has been withdrawn we can only assume that so has the offer for the forgiveness of sin. Such an idea is unthinkable.

While it is true that not everyone receives the forgiveness of sins, the offer still stands. Likewise, while everyone may not receive their healing, the offer still stands.

Yes, all of His promises remain, (2 Corinthians 1:20). In fact, they are more and greater today. The blood of Jesus has given us a new covenant "established upon better promises," (Hebrews 8:6).

The first covenant was filled with promises to heal, and from the beginning God provided healing for all of His people.

There is no clearer declaration of God's willingness to heal than the revelation of one of His seven redemptive names: Jehovah Rapha, *I am the Lord that heals you.*

Exodus 15:26

26 If thou wilt diligently hearken to the voice of the LORD thy God, and wilt do that which is right in his sight, and wilt give ear to his commandments, and keep all his statutes, I will put none of these diseases upon thee, which I have brought upon the Egyptians: for I am the LORD that healeth thee.

If the Old Covenant promised healing how can we say the New Covenant is "established upon better promises" unless healing is available today?

If the promises of the Old Covenant were so powerful that over two million Hebrew children escaped Egypt, "and there was not one feeble person among their tribes," (Psalms 105:37) how can we consider the New Covenant to be "established upon better promises" unless the same and more is available now?

Paul was "persuaded of better things, and of things that accompany salvation," (Hebrews 6:9). There are even greater blessings and benefits that accompany salvation.

Salvation through Jesus Christ delivers us from our sins so that we may be delivered from the temporal evils that are in this present life, (Galatians 1:4).

The Greek word translated salvation, *sozo*, is used in a very broad sense. It concerns the salvation of man from sin, but also deliverance from the consequences of sin.

When Jesus spoke to those who had received healing, He often said, "Go in peace, your faith has healed you," or, more literally, "your faith has saved (*sozo*) you," (Luke

7:50; Luke 18:42).

Salvation from sin, and the healing of our bodies, have both been provided through the great sacrifice of the Son of God. They are available for all and are available now.

God's decision was final and His will was revealed when Jesus "bare our sins in his own body on the tree, that we, being dead to sins, should live unto righteousness: by whose stripes ye were healed," (1 Peter 2:24).

By using the past tense, "by whose stripes ye were healed," Peter places the provision of our healing in the past and removes it from any future doubt or debate. It is an accomplished fact of the atonement.

James declares the same when he instituted the sacrament of healing for the Church, irrevocably linking it with the forgiveness of our sins.

> **James 5:14-16**
> 14 Is any sick among you? let him call for the elders of the church; and let them pray over him, anointing him with oil in the name of the Lord:
> 15 And the prayer of faith shall save the sick, and the Lord shall raise him up; and if he have committed sins, they shall be forgiven him.
> 16 Confess your faults one to another, and pray one for another, that ye may be healed. The effectual fervent prayer of a righteous man availeth much.

Here we see the strong assurance that "the prayer of faith shall save the sick, and the Lord shall raise him up." The promise to heal is just as clear as the promise to forgive: "and if he have committed sins, they shall be forgiven him." It is not reasonable to place faith in God's willingness to forgive while doubting God's willingness to heal. If we remove one, we must remove the other.

Healing is as freely available to the one who believes as the gift of salvation; both are provided by the same sacrifice, and both are included under the same promises. Paul said, "now is the accepted time; behold, now is the time of salvation," (2 Corinthians 6:2).

It is interesting to note that Jesus never commanded His disciples to pray for the sick. Rather, He commanded them to heal the sick, (Matthew 10:8; Luke 9:2; 10:9). His command is another clear declaration of the will of God for any in need of healing. The healing power of God is an ever present source of power available to anyone who will reach out and receive.

Don't wait for God when God is waiting for you. In the face of despair, Jesus told the nobleman to "believe only, and she shall be made whole," (Luke 8:50). He boldly declared the healing of his daughter depended on the father's personal faith to receive. Jesus placed God's power to heal and God's willingness to heal beyond question, while calling on the man to do his part.

Fear not, only believe!

2

The Power of Jesus Christ

In Yerevan, Armenia I preached a sermon on the resurrection of Jesus Christ in an amazing church filled with several hundreds of people. It was Easter Sunday and we were celebrating our living Savior. In the middle of the sermon I cried out, "Jesus is alive!" The anointing of God swept through the building and everyone began to shout praises. I attempted to continue speaking but was forced to stop. I could not go on. An entire section of people were shouting and screaming out of control and they would not stop. Their voices overpowered mine. Something had happened.

"Someone was healed," the interpreter said to me, pointing into the crowd.

Two women stood weeping beside a young teenage girl. Her face shone with surprise and wonder. Together they came to the platform where we quickly learned they were grandmother, mother and daughter. The daughter had been born deaf and dumb, but God had healed her. She could hear!

In the next few minutes she was mouthing sounds, repeating words and to everyone's surprise speaking out loud! The congregation roared with a sea of praise when they heard her repeat the name of Jesus!

No one had prayed for her, no one had touched her. What had happened? How had it happened?

Jesus Christ is Alive!

There have been times when God has opened my eyes into the realm of the spirit and I have been privileged to see Jesus walking through the crowds laying hands on people, healing them.

This is a book about the reality and power of our living Savior. It is filled with instructions on how to receive divine healing, but it is also about much more than physical healing. Healing is only one aspect of the benefits to be found in a personal relationship with Jesus Christ.

By learning to receive God's healing power in the physical realm, we learn how to receive many other benefits that have been promised us. God has blessed us with all spiritual blessings in heavenly places in Christ Jesus, (Ephesians 1:3). These blessings are to be found in "heavenly places" or in the realm of the spirit. There is a physical realm, and there is a spiritual realm. God is spirit, (John 4:24) and He created the physical realm. Recognizing that a spirit created the physical, we can see that the spirit realm is the source, or origin, of all things.

Healing is God's act in the physical realm. There are greater and more powerful miracles that take place in the spirit. The moment of salvation, when a man or woman chooses Jesus Christ as the Lord of their life, is the greatest miracle of all. A man's spirit is reborn and he is made a new creation (2 Corinthians 5:17), a new species of being that never existed before.

Physical things are easier seen and more easily understood. Healing can be a wonderful door to reveal the life of faith as it touches the spiritual facets of life. As we read the Bible, we discover that the faith that saves us is the same faith that heals our body.

> **Matthew 8:2-6**
> 2 And, behold, they brought to him a man sick of the palsy, lying on a bed: and Jesus seeing their faith said unto the sick of the palsy; Son, be of good cheer; thy sins be forgiven thee.
> 3 And, behold, certain of the scribes said within themselves, This man blasphemeth.
> 4 And Jesus knowing their thoughts said, Wherefore think ye evil in your hearts?
> 5 For whether is easier, to say, Thy sins be forgiven thee; or to say, Arise, and walk?
> 6 But that ye may know that the Son of man hath power on earth to forgive sins, (then saith he to the sick of the palsy,) Arise, take up thy bed, and go unto thine house.

Jesus saw their faith, for "Faith is the substance of

things hoped for, the evidence of things not seen," (Hebrews 11:1). If faith is the evidence of what you cannot see, then you must be able to see faith.

Faith is evident. If you can't see it, then is it really faith? How can you see faith? Faith is seen by the actions we take and the words we speak.

Their faith was visible to Jesus by their bold actions to bring their friend through the crowd. They did not act as though they hoped "someday he might be healed." They did not act as though they were taking a chance. They were bold. They were confident. They knew that once in the presence of the Lord Jesus Christ healing would be theirs, and their friend would be set free.

Many believe that God uses sickness to teach you. This is religious tradition, and has done great damage to suffering people everywhere. There is nothing in the Bible to substantiate such an idea.

Notice how Jesus used the man's healing, and not the sickness, as an example to teach the people. The only thing that sickness teaches is that we don't want to be sick. This man's healing became an object lesson for everyone to learn from and receive. In our day many talk about sickness as a lesson. They have it backwards. Jesus saw sickness as a problem and healing as the answer. Let's be careful to approach the lessons of life the way Jesus addressed them.

Jesus said, "That you might know…" (verse six). There was a greater miracle that took place in the spirit – the man's sins had been forgiven. This miracle of the heart could not be seen with their eyes. Jesus displayed His power over sin by showing His power over sickness and disease. He forgave the man his sins, and healed the man of his diseases.

Jesus' power and authority in one area – over the enslaving guilt of sin – was clearly demonstrated by His power over this man's physical disease. It has been the same throughout all time. David gave his praise to God for this same eternal truth.

> **Psalms 103:2-5**
> 2 Bless the LORD, O my soul, and forget not all his benefits:
> 3 Who forgiveth all thine iniquities; who healeth all thy diseases;
> 4 Who redeemeth thy life from destruction; who crowneth thee with lovingkindness and tender mercies;
> 5 Who satisfieth thy mouth with good things; so that thy youth is renewed like the eagle's.

He forgives all our iniquities, and heals all of our diseases!

We are confident to say that the miracle of salvation is far greater than the miracle of healing. We must also realize that if God so freely forgives, and we receive the greater miracle; how much more will He freely heal? Would He withhold the lesser gift?

There was a desperate woman who came to Jesus, pleading that He would heal her daughter. She was not a Jew, and therefore was outside the covenant promises that God had made to His people.

Pay very close attention to this account:

> **Matthew 15:22-28**
>
> 22 And, behold, a woman of Canaan came out of the same coasts, and cried unto him, saying, Have mercy on me, O Lord, thou Son of David; my daughter is grievously vexed with a devil.
>
> 23 But he answered her not a word. And his disciples came and besought him, saying, Send her away; for she crieth after us.
>
> 24 But he answered and said, I am not sent but unto the lost sheep of the house of Israel.
>
> 25 Then came she and worshipped him, saying, Lord, help me.
>
> 26 But he answered and said, It is not meet to take the children's bread, and to cast it to dogs.
>
> 27 And she said, Truth, Lord: yet the dogs eat of the crumbs which fall from their masters' table.
>
> 28 Then Jesus answered and said unto her, O woman, great is thy faith: be it unto thee even as thou wilt. And her daughter was made whole from that very hour.

Jesus said she had great faith. Did you see that? Why was her faith great in His eyes? Because she realized that healing was not a big thing with God.

You may need a miracle right now, and it may seem like the biggest thing in the whole world. Think for a moment. How big is it to God? What does it look like from His perspective? Your mountain is quite small in His eyes, and your healing quite easy to receive.

Receiving God's healing power is easy. You need only a crumb, and God wants you to have the whole loaf!

People often falter when they hear those words but I believe them still. That is really the difference. What you believe about healing will determine what you receive. If you believe healing is difficult, or given only in special cases to a special few, then you have limited yourself and bound yourself to failure.

Your faith is working but in the wrong direction. You believe that you will not be healed. It's time to see from God's own words that it is His will to heal all, and that His promises include you.

I want to encourage you as you read this book. Lay aside what you have thought in the past and approach God's Word with an open and honest heart. Examine the Scriptures verse by verse and see whether these things are so:

Acts 17:11
11 These were more noble than those in Thessalonica, in that they received the word with all readiness of mind, and searched the scriptures daily, whether those things were so.

Remember, God cares deeply about you. Jesus is alive, and the power of Jesus Christ is ever present to heal.

3

Jesus Healed them All

Notice several important passages from Matthew by way of an introduction to the ministry of Jesus:

Matthew 4:23,24

23 And Jesus went about all Galilee, teaching in their synagogues, and preaching the gospel of the kingdom, and healing all manner of sickness and all manner of disease among the people.

24 And his fame went throughout all Syria: and they brought unto him all sick people that were taken with divers diseases and torments, and those which were possessed with devils, and those which were lunatick, and those that had the palsy; and he healed them.

Matthew 9:35
35 And Jesus went about all the cities and villages, teaching in their synagogues, and preaching the gospel of the kingdom, and healing every sickness and every disease among the people.

Matthew 12:15
15 But when Jesus knew it, he withdrew himself from thence: and great multitudes followed him, and he healed them all.

The four Gospels are filled with wonderful descriptions of Jesus healing the sick. Whenever faced with a great multitude of sick people, Jesus "was moved with compassion toward them, and he healed their sick," (Matthew 14:14). Many crowded around Him in order to "touch the hem of his garment: and as many as touched were made perfectly whole," (Matthew 14:36). On one occasion, He asked "that a small ship should wait on him because of the multitude, lest they should throng him. For he had healed many; insomuch that they pressed upon him for to touch him, as many as had plagues," (Mark 3:9-12).

He found little rest and often was exhausted from His ministry of preaching, teaching and healing. Many times, after teaching all the day, He would pray for the sick long into the night, and they often "brought unto him all that were diseased, and them that were possessed with devils. And all the city was gathered together at the door. And he healed many that were sick of divers diseases, and cast out many devils; and suffered not the devils to speak, because they knew him," (Mark 1:32-34).

There were so many sick the people carried "those that were lame, blind, dumb, maimed, and many others, and cast them down at Jesus' feet; and he healed them," (Matthew 15:30). "All they that had any sick with divers diseases brought them unto him; and he laid his hands on every one of them, and healed them," (Luke 4:40).

When news began to spread, people "ran through that whole region round about, and began to carry about in beds those that were sick, where they heard he was. And whithersoever he entered, into villages, or cities, or country, they laid the sick in the streets, and besought him that they might touch if it were but the border of his garment: and as many as touched him were made whole," (Mark 6:55,56).

The crowds grew until "great multitudes followed him; and he healed them," (Matthew 19:2). Even when He entered Jerusalem, "the blind and the lame came to him in the temple; and he healed them," (Matthew 21:14). Always the people "followed him: and he received them, and spake unto them of the kingdom of God, and healed them that had need of healing," (Luke 9:11).

We clearly see that throughout His entire ministry Jesus healed all who came to Him for healing. There is no record of His denying a single one.

We cannot say how many miracles or miraculous healings Jesus ministered. The majority took place in the midst of large crowds. There are approximately twenty-eight references to healings *en masse* where large groups of people came to Jesus and where the multitudes are said to have received healing. In some cases, the healing power of God was so powerful, present and tangible that the sick were being thrown at His feet.

John wrote, "And many other signs truly did Jesus in the presence of his disciples, which are not written in this book," (John 20:30).

The individual cases in Jesus' ministry number twenty-seven. For example, we refer to the woman with the issue of blood, or blind Bartimaeus. These accounts reveal the nature of the sickness, the desperation of the situation, and often display the faith in action that received God's healing power. One gains great insight into Jesus' methods when we examine these individual cases.

There are seventeen specific accounts of healing in the ministry of Jesus, along with seven cases that deal with deliverance from demons. The remaining three accounts describe the raising of the dead. Among the dead we find a child, a young man, and an adult.

We have reason to believe that more than three people were raised from the dead. Jesus implies this in His answer to John the Baptist, (Matthew 11:4,5 and Luke 7:22) where He speaks in a plural sense. Chronologically, at this point in His ministry, only one had been raised. Literally, it reads, "Blind people are seeing, lame people are walking around, leprous people have been cleansed, deaf people are hearing, dead people are being raised up, and poor people are hearing the good news!"

Jesus healed those with fevers, epilepsy, and dropsy. He opened the ears of the deaf, loosed the tongue of the mute, restored the paralyzed, straightened the deformed, cured lepers, the lame, the blind, the impotent, delivered those stricken with insanity or possessed of demons, commanded withered hands to be made whole, stopped the flow of blood, and restored maimed and amputated limbs by creative acts. With great compassion He even laid hands on those with "minor ailments" constantly and everywhere healing "all that had need of healing."

Jesus often dealt with sickness and sin at the same moment, forgiving sin before He spoke His word of healing power. He demonstrated that there is no distance in the spirit, healing many who were far away from His physical presence.

He depended upon the guidance of the Holy Spirit as He ministered in various ways: putting mud on a blind man's eyes, spitting on a deaf man's tongue, or simply leading an afflicted soul away from an atmosphere of unbelief. In some cases He hastened to pray or deliver while at other times He purposely delayed. He allowed two blind men to suffer as they followed Him over a great distance, provoked a sorrowing mother by using harsh words, and often threw the responsibility of healing back upon the desperate individual.

At other times he was enraged against unbelief and brought persecution upon Himself to deliver one "daughter of Israel," or endangered Himself by traveling through stormy seas to deliver one demon possessed man; only to return to the place where He had started.

4

The Question Everyone Asks

I began pastoring a local Church when I was twenty years old. I remember receiving a phone call that same year from a very desperate woman. "Do you believe the Bible? Do you believe that God still heals today?" she asked.

I was astonished to learn that she had called several pastors, and none of them believed that God would heal in answer to prayer. They had given her various reasons why miracles were not for today, and one tried to convince her that sickness and disease were methods God sometimes uses to teach us. She was told that she should accept this sickness as being the will of God. None of them even offered to pray with her.

Her husband was very ill. She, and a few of her friends,

had prayed but no answer had come. His condition had not improved, but actually grown worse.

"Pastor," she asked, "Is it God's will for my husband to be sick? Why doesn't God answer me?"

My heart went out to this woman. She had prayed for her husband's healing but wasn't sure if she was praying correctly. What she read in the Bible wasn't what she was experiencing in her life. Even her spiritual leaders were denying her hope in a God who heals today. She didn't know what to do.

"Sister," I answered, "don't be discouraged. Remember that you can never determine the will of God by the circumstances or by your experience. God's will is revealed in the Bible. Each of His promises are a revelation of His will for us. Let's look at what the Bible says."

I went on to show her an illustration from Mark chapter nine, beginning in verse fourteen:

> **Mark 9:14-18**
> 14 And when he came to his disciples, he saw a great multitude about them, and the scribes questioning with them.
> 15 And straightway all the people, when they beheld him, were greatly amazed, and running to him saluted him.
> 16 And he asked the scribes, What question ye with them?
> 17 And one of the multitude answered and said, Master, I have brought unto thee my son, which hath a dumb spirit;

> 18 And wheresoever he taketh him, he teareth him: and he foameth, and gnasheth with his teeth, and pineth away: and I spake to they disciples that they should cast him out; and they could not.

At this point in His ministry, Jesus encountered a large group of people asking the religious leaders certain questions. These questions are still being asked in our day by concerned people all over the world.

What is the Question?

When the crowd saw Jesus they immediately ran to him and gave him their full attention. He asked the scribes, "What is the question?"

A man spoke up from the crowd and explained the situation. He shared about the terrible condition of his son, how prayer was made by Jesus' disciples, but nothing had changed. "I asked your disciples to cast out this evil spirit, but they could not."

Have you ever noticed that? Jesus' disciples prayed and failed to receive an answer. Men closest to the Master failed. They prayed and nothing happened!

We are never told what questions were asked about this situation, or even what the disciples might have said concerning their inability to deliver the boy from Satan's power. Whatever questions they asked, the debate had continued until a large crowd gathered. I think we can imagine what some of the questions might have been, and even what some of the religious answers may have been.

Perhaps you have asked similar questions yourself?
> *Why weren't my prayers answered?*
> *Is it God's will to heal me?*
> *Is it God's will to heal all the time?*
> *Why didn't healing come?*
> *Are miracles for today?*
> *Is God trying to teach me something?*
> *Am I being punished for my sin?*

And what answers have you heard before?
> *Sometimes God answers yes, sometimes no.*
> *It isn't God's will to heal everyone.*
> *Miracles passed away with the apostles.*
> *God has a purpose in your suffering.*
> *You never know what God is going to do.*

We have come to expect Jesus to offer different answers than many religious people. Let's read further and see how Jesus responds.

> **Mark 9:19-27**
> 19 He answereth him, and saith, O faithless generation, how long shall I be with you? How long shall I suffer you? bring him unto me.
> 20 And they brought him unto him: and when he saw him, straightway the spirit tare him; and he fell on the ground and wallowed foaming.
> 21 And he asked his father, How long is it ago since this came unto him? And he said, Of a child.

22 And ofttimes it hath cast him into the fire, and into the waters, to destroy him: but if thou canst do any thing, have compassion on us, and help us.

23 Jesus said unto him, If thou canst believe, all things are possible to him that believeth.

24 And straightway the father of the child cried out, and said with tears, Lord, I believe; help thou mine unbelief.

25 When Jesus saw that the people came running together, he rebuked the foul spirit, saying unto him, Thou dumb and deaf spirit, I charge thee, come out of him, and enter no more into him.

26 And the spirit cried, and rent him sore, and came out of him: and he was as one dead; insomuch that many said, He is dead.

27 But Jesus took him by the hand, and lifted him up; and he arose.

The Bible everywhere and always shows us that Jesus is a healer. From the beginning of His ministry He "went about all Galilee, teaching in their synagogues, and preaching the gospel of the kingdom, and healing all manner of sickness and all manner of disease among the people," (Matthew 4:23). He was always busy "healing every sickness and every disease among the people," (Matthew 9:35). Whenever people came to him, "He received them, and spake unto them of the kingdom of God, and healed them that had need of healing," (Luke 9:11). Everywhere he was "moved with compassion and healed the sick," (Matthew 14:14).

His healing ministry became so consistent that

eventually the Scribes and Pharisees waited for him to heal in order to accuse Him of breaking their laws, (Mark 3:2-5). Think about that! His enemies counted on the fact that He would heal the sick.

Imagine what would have happened if Jesus had not ministered to this child. What if this poor father had gone home after the disciples' failure to heal the boy? What would people have said then?

They would have said the same thing many are saying today – that God no longer heals, that it is His will for people to be sick, and that miracles are not to be expected. They would have based their understanding of the will of God on their own experience and on their own failure to bring results.

Sometimes we miss it when we pray. Sometimes our praying is not effective. James says that "you ask, and receive not, because you ask amiss…" (James 4:3). If the disciples prayed and failed to receive, what should we do when our prayers go unanswered? Should we quietly assume that it was never God's will to grant our request? Or could it be that we have lessons to learn about the life of prayer?

We need to learn to pray correctly for prayer was never meant to go unanswered. The reason for prayer is answers, and the answer to our prayers is a source of abundant joy. Jesus said, "Hitherto have ye asked nothing in my name: ask, and ye shall receive, that your joy may be full" (John 16:24).

I have seen people pray for the sick and when healing did not come say dismissively "It must not be the will of God to heal..."

Do you see the pride in that statement? Can they pray better than Peter, more powerfully than John, with more thunder than James? Are they more spiritually mature than the disciples? Do their prayers never fail?

Jesus Didn't Think So

The disciples had prayed and healing did not come. Did that mean it was God's will for the boy to be sick? Jesus didn't think so. He plainly revealed that it was God's will to heal the boy. He broke through the barriers of unanswered prayer and demonstrated the will of God by healing the boy.

Later, the disciples admitted their failure and asked Jesus, "Why couldn't we cast the evil spirit out of the boy?" (verse 28) That was the real question that needed asking, and one that we need to ask when faced with similar difficulties.

They never attributed any failure to God, made no comment about God's will, but looked to themselves for the source of failure. They were honest men.

Sometimes we miss it and God is not to be blamed.

You can never determine the will of God by your experience, but only by the living Word of God. God's promises were given to provide the ability to change our circumstances. Many go through life accepting their condition as being from the hand of God. They live defeated lives when they could receive the healing power of God through His many promises.

It's time we stopped covering up our failures with religious excuses. Sometimes we miss it. Sometimes its painful to accept the truth. When healing doesn't come or our prayers are not answered, we need to realize that something has to change. We know that God does not change, so the changes have to begin with us.

Paul talked about a "fight of faith," (1 Timothy 6:12). Looking at the New Testament you see that the greatest miracles came to people who were willing to fight for the will of God to be established in their life. They did not fold their hands and accept what life had given them. They did not sit quietly when Satan brought sickness, disease or even death to their homes.

When a man lie dying, his four friends tore up the roof of the house to bring him to Jesus, (Mark 2:4,5). The ruler of the synagogue threw away his reputation for the sake of his daughter when he knelt at Jesus feet, asking Him to come and lay His hands on her so she might live, (Mark 5:22,23). The Syrophenician woman would not leave until she had obtained one small crumb from the Master's table, (Matthew 15:22-28). When people told him to be quiet, blind Bartimaeus cried out even more, until the Son of David came and had mercy on him, and healed his blind eyes, (Mark 10:46-52).

In each of these examples Jesus refers to their "fight of faith." Looking at the four friends we read that "Jesus saw their faith;" and to the ruler of the synagogue, He declares, "Fear not: believe only, and she shall be made whole." To the Syrophenician woman, Jesus says "great is thy faith: be it unto thee even as thou wilt" and to blind Bartimaeus, "Go thy way; thy faith hath made thee whole."

Desperate people took drastic measures and received dramatic results. I believe you have this same fight of faith working in your heart right now. That's why you are reading this book. That's why you have opened your heart and your mind to learn what the Bible has to say about divine healing. That's why there is a hunger in your heart to know the truth.

And that's why you will be healed.

5

If You Can Believe

Faith begins where the will of God is known. Faith in God is based on the integrity of His Word. Before anyone can have faith to receive healing they must be confident that God has promised to heal.

Miracles are not accidents, but the result of intelligently cooperating with the revealed will of God as found in the Bible. The purpose of the Word of God is to give an intelligent idea of God's will.

The integrity of the Word is the basis of our faith and we know that "faith cometh by hearing, and hearing by the Word of God," (Romans 10:17). If we lack faith, it can be said that we lack the knowledge of God's will as revealed in the Bible.

It really isn't a faith problem, it's a problem of not having sufficient knowledge of God's Word to produce the faith we need.

Jesus said, "If you can believe, all things are possible to him that believes," (Mark 9:23). But faith cannot exist where the will of God is not known. You simply cannot believe beyond what you know the will of God to be. Before faith can be confident and steadfast you need to be free from all uncertainty and doubt.

By spending time feeding on the Word we nourish our faith on his promises and faith grows. What He has promised He will perform. He is watching over His Word to fulfill it on our behalf, (Jeremiah 1:12).

Learning to Receive

In my first year of pastoring, I saw an interesting example of how simple it can be to receive healing from God when we acquaint ourselves with His will. During our Sunday morning services a woman would slip quietly into our small Church building and sit in the back. I saw that she carried a Bible and followed the teaching by reading along at every verse I would mention. She wrote notes into a small book, but as soon as I had finished teaching she would quickly leave.

I asked several of the people about her, but no one seemed to know who she was. This continued for several weeks. She would come after the service had already started, listen attentively, and then leave before the service was over.

But one day she didn't leave. As I finished teaching, I invited people to come forward to receive prayer for healing. Without hesitation, she stood up and marched down to the front of the Church. She was prayed for, along with several others, and then she quickly left the building before anyone could speak with her. I honestly can say that I didn't feel anything special when I prayed for her, or that God had moved in any special way.

The next Sunday I was surprised to see her arrive at Church early, and with her husband at her side. Her face was bright and full of joy. I knew in my heart that something had happened, and I was eager to talk to her.

After the service, she approached me with her husband. "Pastor," she said, "can we speak with you?"

"Of course," I said, and she went on to tell me her story. She had been diagnosed by medical experts as having a serious heart condition. A heart transplant had been suggested, but she didn't want to do that. They had said that she could die at any moment. She might be walking normally about the house and drop over dead without any warning. Of course, this made her seek the Lord more than ever before.

She had come to the Church with certain questions in her mind about healing. She told me that whenever she would have a specific question the sermon that week would contain the answer. It's important that you attend a Church where the Spirit of God is free to move and reveal the Word of God. You know you are home if that's where your mail is delivered!

Over time she realized that it was God's will to heal, and more important she realized that it was God's will to heal her. She had a growing confidence in her heart that if she came forward for prayer, God would give her a new heart. She told her husband she was going to go forward for prayer and be healed.

And that's exactly what happened. After she had received prayer, she made another appointment with the same doctors. They couldn't explain it, but her heart was now normal. One said, "It's as if you have a completely new heart." They took new x-rays and showed her the difference. They didn't know what to say.

God Gave Her a New Heart

Here was a woman who had received the Word of God into her heart, believed it, and received the very thing she prayed.

What she experienced is exactly what happened in Mark chapter five. Notice how this woman received God's healing power.

Mark 5:25-34

25 And a certain woman, which had an issue of blood twelve years,

26 And had suffered many things of many physicians, and had spent all that she had, and was nothing bettered, but rather grew worse,

27 When she had heard of Jesus, came in the press behind, and touched his garment.

28 For she said, If I may touch but his clothes, I shall be whole.

29 And straightway the fountain of her blood was dried up; and she felt in her body that she was healed of that plague.

30 And Jesus, immediately knowing in himself that virtue had gone out of him, turned him about in the press, and said, Who touched my clothes?

31 And his disciples said unto him, Thou seest the multitude thronging thee, and sayest thou, Who touched me?
32 And he looked round about to see her that had done this thing.
33 But the woman fearing and trembling, knowing what was done in her, came and fell down before him, and told him all the truth.
34 And he said unto her, Daughter, thy faith hath made thee whole; go in peace, and be whole of thy plague.

What Jesus Didn't Say

This woman had nearly lost hope. Every natural effort had failed. Her money was gone and still her condition had not changed. The Bible says she was growing worse. Then she touched the hem of his garment and was healed. Before we look at what Jesus said about the woman's healing, let's look at what he did not say.

Did you notice that Jesus didn't say "I healed you."

In fact, as we read this portion of Scripture we are forced to realize that Jesus didn't know the woman was there until after she was healed. Jesus stopped to look around and find who had touched him. He knew someone had been healed, but who? We know that Jesus is the healer, and we know that the woman would not have been healed apart from Jesus, but Jesus Himself took no credit for this healing.

Did you notice that Jesus didn't say "My power healed you."

He asked his disciples, "who touched me" because He had felt healing power leave His body. Certainly the healing power that left His body went into the woman. Certainly it was His healing power that healed the woman, but Jesus never said "My power healed you."

Did you notice that Jesus didn't say "God healed you."

We know that God is the healer, and that ultimately God was the healer in this case as in all cases. Some people think that God heals from time to time, and in an arbitrary fashion. We need to realize that there are specific ways, and even laws, that determine the healing power of God. But Jesus didn't say God healed her.

What did Jesus say?

He said, "Daughter, thy faith hath made thee whole; go in peace, and be whole of thy plague." Jesus placed the result of her healing on the simple fact that she had believed. Her faith was responsible, and because of her faith she was healed.

But where did she get this faith to be healed?

She Heard of Jesus

"When she had heard of Jesus, she came in the press behind, and touched his garment." Remember that "faith cometh by hearing, and hearing by the Word of God," (Romans 10:17). What the woman heard gave her the faith to receive.

This should make us ask a question about what we have been hearing where faith and healing are concerned.

No wonder we don't see more healings and miracles in

our day. Do you think she would have forced her way through the crowd if she had heard that miracles had passed away? Do you think she would have touched the hem of his garment if she had been taught that God uses sickness and disease to teach her lessons? We have heard religious traditions for so long until they have robbed us of our faith, and made the Word of God ineffective in our life, (Matthew 15:6).

Jesus has commanded us to preach the Gospel. The Greek word for Gospel means "good news." Many are preaching "bad news" and not "good news." Many read the Bible to find verses that condemn themselves. They are so focused on the negative they cannot see good when it comes.

Jesus was a Preacher

Everywhere Jesus went, He preached the Gospel. We need to remember that Jesus was a preacher. The people came to hear Him, until "many were gathered together, insomuch that there was no room to receive them, no, not so much as about the door: and he preached the word unto them," (Mark 2:2). Luke tells us that He saturated an entire region with His teaching by "preaching in the synagogues of Galilee," (Luke 4:44). When asked about His ministry, Jesus included the preaching of the Gospel. "Go your way," He said, "and tell John what things ye have seen and heard; how that the blind see, the lame walk, the lepers are cleansed, the deaf hear, the dead are raised, to the poor the gospel is preached," (Luke 7:22).

He pointed to a new and higher importance of preaching, showing how it surpassed the Old Covenant, as "The law and the prophets were until John: since that time the kingdom of God is preached, and every man presseth into it," (Luke 16:16).

Wherever He went there was one message that He always preached. Peter said that Jesus preached this same message through all of Judea. Its main theme was how "God anointed Jesus of Nazareth with the Holy Ghost and with power: who went about doing good, and healing all that were oppressed of the devil; for God was with him," (Acts 10:37,38).

He said that this message was preached from the very start of Jesus' ministry, beginning at Galilee immediately after He was baptized of John. It was the foundation of Jesus' preaching and can be seen running through the pages of the four gospels.

> **Matthew 4:23,24**
> 23 And Jesus went about all Galilee, teaching in their synagogues, and preaching the gospel of the kingdom, and healing all manner of sickness and all manner of disease among the people.
> 24 And his fame went throughout all Syria: and they brought unto him all sick people that were taken with divers diseases and torments, and those which were possessed with devils, and those which were lunatick, and those that had the palsy; and he healed them.

This must be what the woman heard about Jesus. It was the message Jesus shared everywhere he went: teaching, preaching and healing. It would have been on the lips of all those who had heard Him.

Faith comes by hearing the Word of God, and faith for healing comes from hearing what the Word of God has to say about divine healing. What did she learn from this message Jesus preached?

She would have learned that He was anointed with the Holy Spirit and with power. The Holy Spirit is the giver of gifts, including the gifts of healing and the working of miracles, (1 Corinthians 12:9,10). He was also anointed with power, just as this power left His body when she touched the hem of His garment. She would have learned that Jesus healed all, not just some; and she would have learned that it was God's will to heal her. She would have learned that sickness and disease is the oppression of the devil. She would have learned that sickness is not from God.

She heard the Word of God, faith came into her heart, and she acted on what she believed. She said, "If I may touch but his clothes, I shall be whole."

What She Said Came to Pass

Paul said this is the spirit of faith: "I believed, and therefore have I spoken; we also believe, and therefore speak," (2 Corinthians 4:13).

The spirit of faith declares that you will speak what you believe. You can locate people by listening to what they say. You can determine their faith by what they speak. The woman said she would be healed when she touched his clothes because that is what she believed, and what she said came to pass. She received the exact thing she said.

As you read the Bible, you will learn the importance of words, the power of saying what God says. "Life and death are in the power of the tongue," (Proverbs 18:21). Your words determine in a large way what you receive from heaven. Many pray one thing and say another. They pray for healing and moments later speak of how bad they feel, how their condition is not improving. You can't pray in faith and speak in doubt at the same time.

What you say reveals what you believe. Jesus said, "Out of the abundance of the heart the mouth speaks," (Matthew 12:34). When you have the Word in your heart in abundance you will speak the Word in the face of contrary circumstances and those circumstances will change.

She said, "If I may touch but his clothes, I shall be whole."

She Acted on Her Faith

Faith by itself does nothing. Without corresponding actions to what we believe, then faith is dead and unproductive.

James 2:17, 18 (Weymouth translation) "So also faith, if it is unaccompanied by obedience, has no life in it — so long as it stands alone. Nay, some one will say, "You have faith, I have actions: prove to me your faith apart from corresponding actions and I will prove mine to you by my actions."

Many have faith in their heart, but their actions do not correspond. They believe they are healed, but their actions are based on what they see or feel. They feel sick, so they remain in bed. If the woman had acted on what she felt, she never would have forced her way through a crowd. It was by acting on what she believed, in spite of what she felt, that caused her to reach out and touch the hem of his garment.

It is possible to believe in the heart, but to act "from the head" and fail to receive.

Abraham knew the natural possibilities of having a child, but he chose to consider God's promises as a higher priority than what he could see or feel. He based his actions on what he believed, not on what he thought or felt.

> **Romans 4:19-21**
> 19 And being not weak in faith, he considered not his own body now dead, when he was about an hundred years old, neither yet the deadness of Sara's womb:
> 20 He staggered not at the promise of God through unbelief; but was strong in faith, giving glory to God;
> 21 And being fully persuaded that, what he had promised, he was able also to perform.

Faith is never effective until it is released. Remember, there are primarily two ways we release faith – by what we say and by what we do. Our words and our actions release our faith.

She Made a Demand on His Ability

By speaking her faith, "If I may touch but his clothes, I shall be whole" – and by acting on what she believed –

she came in the press behind, and touched his garment – this woman made a demand on Jesus' ability.

She determined when and where she would be healed. By releasing her faith through what she said and what she did, she received the healing power of God. The healing power of God is an ever present source of power available to anyone who will reach out and receive.

Many are waiting for God to do something. They are waiting for a vision or a dream, or some sign from heaven that they will be healed. They are waiting for a Prophet to prophesy, or for a miracle to appear.

This woman didn't wait, she reached out with a faith that takes, and she moved the hand of God. She touched the hem of His garment:

> **Luke 8:45,46**
> 45 And Jesus said, Who touched me? When all denied, Peter and they that were with him said, Master, the multitude throng thee and press thee, and sayest thou, Who touched me?
> 46 And Jesus said, Somebody hath touched me: for I perceive that virtue is gone out of me.

Jesus was conscious that the anointing power of God had gone out of him. Someone had touched him, he said.

But an entire crowd was touching him.

Did you notice that? An entire crowd was touching him, thronging him, but the touch of one woman was somehow different. Her touch was the touch of faith.

Others could have received. Surely there were other

sick people in this crowd of people, but only one received. Jesus said, "Someone deliberately touched me, for I felt healing power go out from me."

When you speak your faith and act on what you believe you establish a point of contact. Touching the hem of Jesus' garment was the point of contact for the woman to receive her healing. Jesus was not aware of her presence until after she had touched him and made a demand on the healing anointing that was on His life. He had been anointed with the Holy Ghost and with power. The woman drew that anointing into her physical body and was healed.

Jesus said, "your faith has made you well."

Now if her faith could make her well, your faith can make you well. She spoke her faith, and acted on what she believed. She touched the hem of Jesus garment as a point of contact and released her faith.

As you feed on God's Word faith will come. As faith rises in your heart, speak His promises continually.

Make the same demand on His ability and even as she was healed, you will find the power of God moving in your body and bringing total healing and health.

6

Miraculous Love

It has been said that faith begins where the will of God is known.

> **Mark 1:40-42**
> 40 And there came a leper to him, beseeching him, and kneeling down to him, and saying unto him, If thou wilt, thou canst make me clean.
> 41 And Jesus, moved with compassion, put forth his hand, and touched him, and saith unto him, I will; be thou clean.
> 42 And as soon as he had spoken, immediately the leprosy departed from him, and he was cleansed.

When the leper approached Jesus he declared his faith in God's ability to heal, but expressed doubt in God's willingness. Men sooner believe in miraculous power than miraculous love. Modern theology magnifies the power of God more than it magnifies His compassion; His power more than it does the great fact that His exceeding great power is exercised towards us who believe.

The Bible does not say that God is power, but it does say that God is love, (1 John 4:16). We are instructed to know and believe in His great love. It is not what God can do, but what He yearns to do that inspires faith.

We need to make a distinction between the ability of God and the will of God. Many have faith in His ability, but fail to receive healing because they are unsure of His willingness to heal them personally. They acknowledge that God is a healer, and even that He has healed others; but they cannot boldly answer the question: "will God heal me?"

When they hear testimonies of others who have received healing their faith shrivels and they feel isolated and alone. Instead of being uplifted and encouraged they are depressed and discouraged. Their doubts are based on a sense of unworthiness. Many people struggle with feelings of inadequacy and live with the consciousness of sin and failure. If they are honest with themselves they would say that they do not deserve to be healed.

Perhaps the leper looked at himself that way. His disease had made him an outcast of society. He was declared unclean, and according to Levitical law was forbidden to approach people.

We can see that it was an act of faith just for this man to come to Jesus.

Jesus responded to the leper's question about God's

will by showing His compassion. The love of God is the will of God in action. God's will always reveals His love towards man.

Jesus touched the man who was untouchable.

Jesus said to the leper, "I will; be thou clean," and immediately the leprosy departed from him and he was healed. As soon as the love of God was expressed, and as soon as the man had an understanding of the will of God, he received his healing.

What can you say about God's love towards you?

Has God made His will known concerning the healing of your body today?

God's Will Made Known

A man's will is revealed by his words and by his actions.

It is no different with God. Jesus acted in compassion toward the leper by touching him and He answered without hesitation, "I will."

The provision of healing made for the leper is the same made for you and I. Jesus, who touched and healed the leper, "took our infirmities, and bare our sicknesses" when He hung upon the cross, (Matthew 8:17) and it is "by his stripes ye were healed," (1 Peter 2:24).

This is an Eternal "I will" spoken for all who will believe.

Remember, He has said,

> **3 John 2**
> 2 Beloved, I wish above all things that thou mayest prosper and be in health, even as thy soul prospereth.

The heart of our Father is filled with compassion for His children. You are His beloved. We know that John was inspired by the Holy Spirit, (2 Timothy 3:16) and what he wrote was a revelation of God's will for all. God's will is for you to prosper and be in health.

Many go to great lengths and try to explain why a Bible promise such as this does not apply to them or is not valid for today. There are those who condemn themselves and even search for a reason why God's promises do not work for them. Their vain reasoning is actually discussed in this one Bible promise. Their failure to receive and even their attempt to reject divine healing is explained when John said, "even as your soul prospers."

Their soul has not prospered to see God's willingness to heal them now.

God's will can only be embraced as our soul prospers, or as our mind is renewed on the Word of God. Many fail to receive God's will personally because they have failed to renew their thinking in line with Scriptural truth. After salvation, the most important thing for you to do is renew your mind on the Word of God.

> **Romans 12:2**
> 2 And be not conformed to this world: but be ye transformed by the renewing of your mind, that ye may prove what is that good, and acceptable, and perfect, will of God.

You cannot "prove" (the Greek reads, *experience*) the will of God until your mind is renewed. When Jesus touched the leper, and spoke His will, the mind of the leper was renewed to receive God's promises. He had known of God's power to heal but he was now confident in God's eager willingness. He learned that God is good.

It is the goodness of God that leads to repentance, (Romans 2:4). Repentance means to change your mind, or to change the way you think. We often think of repentance in connection with receiving forgiveness, but repentance refers to more than sin. It means to change your direction by changing the way you think. God's goodness will change the way you think. It will renew your mind and enable you to experience His will.

With Long Life Will He Satisfy You

Some years ago I received a phone call just before beginning to teach in a small home group. My father had called to tell me that my grandfather had been taken to the hospital. He had suffered a severe heart attack and the doctors did not expect him to live through the night. He was paralyzed on one side, and then after suffering a stroke, he fell unconscious.

I told my father that I would leave immediately and come to the hospital, but he said "No, finish your bible study and then call us here."

We gathered in our small group and began to pray. I found myself praying a very religious prayer. It went something like this: "Lord, you've given my grandfather a good life. He's over seventy years old. If it's your time to take him Lord, let him go quickly." I'm sure I was just saying phrases I had heard before by others in similar situations.

While I was praying, my spirit within me became heavy

and with every additional word I felt more and more uncomfortable. I knew this to mean that I had grieved the Holy Spirit. I felt like I had done something terribly wrong.

What I felt, or sensed, was the reaction of my spirit within me to what I was saying. The Holy Spirit bears witness with our spirit (Romans 8:16) not with our mind or our emotions. The Holy Spirit and the Word of God are one and they agree, (1 John 5:7). When we disagree with the Word we are disagreeing with the Spirit. When we walk or speak contrary to the Word we are walking contrary to the Holy Spirit. The more time you spend meditating in the Word and communing with the Spirit the more sensitive you will become to His will and His way.

I knew what the Word of God had to say about my grandfather's condition. I had read it many times and had even committed it to memory. I had renewed my mind to think God's thoughts after Him. What were God's thoughts about this situation?

These Scriptures came to my mind:

> **Psalms 91:10,16**
> 10 There shall no evil befall thee, neither shall any plague come nigh thy dwelling.
> 16 With long life will I satisfy him, and shew him my salvation.

In my heart I knew my grandfather was not satisfied, and I knew it wasn't right that he die sick, nor that he go to heaven without saying goodbye to his family whom he loved.

I stopped speaking right in the middle of my prayer. I

made everyone open their eyes and look up. I said, "I apologize. Please forgive me, but I have been praying wrong. It's not God's will that he die sick. Let's pray again."

We joined our hands again and prayed. "Father," I asked, "forgive me for my unbelief. I know it's not your will that my grandfather die sick. If it's his time to die, heal him first, and then let him go home happy. In the name of Jesus, Amen."

I realized the people in that small group thought my actions were a little out of the ordinary from what they had experienced in the past. They weren't sure what to think about my simple approach to what God has said in His Word. I have always thought that God shouldn't have promised anything if He didn't mean to back it up. I have known God to always honor His Word.

Within the hour my grandfather sat up in bed completely healed.

Do you see how renewing the mind changed the way we approached the prayer? If we had prayed a traditional prayer, and not given the priority to the Word of God to change the very way we think, then he would not have been healed.

The next day he was discharged from the hospital and he went home in better health than he had experienced for many years. In fact, some years before this incident he had lost his equilibrium and could not walk without a cane. He left the cane in the hospital room and walked confidently from that time on. He had lost most of his hearing, but when he rose from that hospital bed God had restored his hearing, also.

He told my father an amazing story. While he lay on the hospital bed unconscious, machines keeping him alive, his spirit went to heaven to be with God.

He said that he had been walking down a beautiful forest path when he came to a large gate. A man of huge stature opened the gate and greeted him. My grandfather said that he was the tallest man he had ever seen. He told my grandfather that he could enter and enjoy this wonderful place of paths and lakes and streams. My grandfather had lived his life as a farmer and spent much of his time in the forest hunting and fishing. I am sure this would have been heaven for him.

He also said that there were many people there and everyone was praising God. My grandfather had spent his life in a very traditional Church singing traditional hymns. He said to my father, "They are just like you, you know. Everyone there was raising their hands in the air and worshiping the Lord!" He spent some time walking beside beautiful lakes and worshiping the Lord. He said it was an indescribable experience.

While he was enjoying this place of wonder, the tall man from the gate approached him again. I am sure that he was an angel. He said to my grandfather, "You have to go back. You will go back for two weeks and then you will return here."

Like waking from a dream, my grandfather sat up in the hospital bed completely well. God had answered prayer, and for the next two weeks he spent his time saying goodbye to his many friends. He settled his financial affairs and made arrangements just like he was going on a long journey.

And exactly two weeks later he died in his own bed, lying on his side with his hands folded under his cheek. There was a smile on his face and the peace of God in the room. He had passed during his sleep and returned to his reward.

God's will for you is good. What He has done for one, He will do for all. As you meditate on His promises, and discern His character as revealed in the Bible, you will begin to think differently about your personal ability to receive from God.

Only when we think God's thoughts and speak God's Word do we experience God's will in every way.

You know that you are loved by a faithful Father. You know that you have a right to receive what He has abundantly provided. You know that He loves you more than any earthly Father. He wants you to prosper and be in health. You know that it is the will of God to heal you now.

7

The Priority of the Word

There is a difference between truth and fact, as there is a difference between faith and experience.

Jesus faulted the Jewish leaders for not handling the Scriptures correctly: they thought they had eternal life, but the Scriptures point back to Jesus, and they refused to accept him or follow him. Here is where they failed — for, "if you had *believed* Moses you would have *believed* in me, for Moses wrote of me. But if you don't *believe* his writings, how will you *believe* my words?" (John 5:39-47).

Four times Jesus used the word, *believe*. This should be startling to us all. People can study and memorize and mold their life around the Scriptures, as the Pharisees and Saducees had done, and still fail to *believe* them. Failing to believe them, they also fail to understand them.

Many try to substitute a spiritual encounter or

experience for faith, looking for a miracle or a sign or a wonder to change someone's heart. As marvelous as they are, miracles never build faith. Their main purpose is to point people to the Word of God — and then, when a man faces the Word of God; or rather, when the Word of God confronts the man; then, and only then, does faith rise in the heart.

"Faith comes by hearing, and hearing by the Word of God," (Romans 10:17).

Remember that the Hebrew used repetition to show emphasis. Hearing and hearing is being emphasized. Paul is making a point we dare not miss. Joshua said, "This book of the law shall not depart out of thy mouth, but thou shalt meditate therein day and night…" (Joshua 1:8). Again, the Psalmist writes, "in his law doth he meditate day and night…" (Psalms 1:2). You may think I am repeating myself, but you need to understand how important it is: *faith comes by hearing the Word of God, and only by hearing the Word of God.*

The priority of the Word in our lives cannot be underestimated. We dare not treat the Bible as a common book for it is the living Word of God. How we treat the Word of God is exactly how we treat the Father, and respect for one is respect for the other.

Your respect for me, or for any man, is measured in what respect you place in my words; how much more when we talk of a living God, and the living Word of God? You cannot disregard a man's word and expect anyone to think otherwise about your disregard and disrespect for the person. If you scorn a man's word, everyone will assume you scorn the man himself.

The Priority of the Word

Your spiritual walk begins and stands on this point. How do you regard the Bible, what respect do you place in the Word of God? This is the measure of your respect for God. If you don't spend time in the Word, it's clear you don't have time for God.

Do you remember the rich man in death, how he pleaded with Abraham to send someone back from the dead to warn his brothers? He did not want to see them suffer a similar fate, so he begged Abraham that they would not come to that place of torment.

Abraham's answer was clear: "They have Moses and the prophets; let them hear them." (Luke 16:29)

The man pleaded again, and here his thought is parallel with the thinking of so many in our day: if someone is raised from the dead, if they see a miracle, then the people will repent and believe. This places a higher regard on experience than truth, don't you see it? When we look for experiences and miracles to produce faith we are actually showing a lack of respect for the Word of God that we possess. We have it now, here in this book, the Bible.

The Word alone is sufficient. You hold in your hands the key to build faith into your heart and life, to obtain the promises of God, to pray and see results.

Miracles don't produce faith; faith produces miracles.

Abraham said, "They have a Bible, let them read it." For many this sounds hard and cold. Doesn't he care? they ask. Why doesn't he do something more? This reveals their lack of understanding of the power of the Word, and their lack of priority of it's role in their life. When the Word of God holds its proper place in a person's life, then what Abraham said makes perfect sense, and lifts the spirit.

Yes! they have the Word — the living Word of God is here now — and the Word of God working in a man or woman's heart is more powerful than if someone rises from the dead to declare the realities of life after death!

Jesus insisted on our need to choose the Word of God above all else in life, and our right to do so. I have learned that in every successful Christian life, there is a point in time when that person had to choose the Word, they had to make it their first priority.

Mary chose the Word of God, and placed a higher priority on sitting at the feet of Jesus and hearing his teaching than attending to her duties and responsibilities. When her sister Martha complained to the Lord, she appealed to common sense and reason. I imagine she was surprised at Jesus response: "But one thing is needful: and Mary hath chosen that good part, which shall not be taken away from her," (Luke 10:42).

Is this, perhaps, the one thing that is needed in your life? You will need to choose, just as Mary chose, in the face of many other things calling for your attention.

Jesus told a parable once, about a King preparing a banquet and inviting people to attend, (Luke 14:16ff). Immediately, the excuses began: for one, about his business, another about his needs, another about his relationships. There is no mention of the Enemy here, no work of Satan. The only thing that kept them from the banquet table were the excuses of common, everyday life.

I have found the greatest enemies to a strong faith life are the common distractions of life that steal one's time from the Word. Guard it at any cost. Keep it as the

The Priority of the Word

highest priority in your life. Don't let anything take you away from your time with the Lord, and when you sit at his feet, attend to His every Word as if it were your last.

Here it is again:

> **Proverbs 4:20-23**
> 20 My son, attend to my words; incline thine ear unto my sayings.
> 21 Let them not depart from thine eyes; keep them in the midst of thine heart.
> 22 For they are life unto those that find them, and health to all their flesh.
> 23 Keep thy heart with all diligence; for out of it are the issues of life

Guard your heart. It's easier to lose here than you might imagine. Many things call for your attention, and if you are not careful you will let things slip. It's a good thing to examine yourself from time to time, to see if you have let go of the Word of God. If you find it to be true, return again to the former disciplines. Get up a bit early, stay up a bit late, but by all means get back into the Book.

I find people repenting often for this or that sin, but if the truth were told, this is where repentance should begin. Repent for your disregard of the Word of God, repent for not spending the time you know you ought, feeding on His Word and meditating on His promises. A victory here, placing the Word of God as the first priority in your life, will bring victory everywhere. One can never expect a victory that overcomes the world without faith (1 John 5:4), and one can never expect faith without time in the Word, much time given to the careful reading and meditation of God's Word.

If the devil can keep you busy repenting and weeping over the small sins of life, he knows he can keep you from going back to what really matters. He pushes you into condemnation and guilt and depression and away from time in God's Word. Do you see it? He is afraid you will return to the Word of God, build a strong and solid foundation under your feet, where the storms of life cannot touch you, (Matthew 7:24-27). You have to choose the Word of God, feed on the word, act on it, and faith will grow. This is the victory that overcomes the world.

It is the one thing needful, Jesus said.

8

God's Word is Medicine

Jesus said that His words are "spirit and life," (John 6:63). They impart life to a man's spirit before they educate the man's mind, or his soul. Jesus did not say His words are soul and life. He said, spirit and life.

Spirit and soul are quite different. The spirit is not the soul anymore than the soul is the body.

Things that pertain to the spirit are as distinct and separate from things that pertain to the soul, just as things that pertain to the physical body are distinct and separate from things that pertain to the spirit.

It is the living Word of God that reveals the difference of these three aspects of human nature, (Hebrews 4:12). Sometimes by separating Man's nature for the sake of curiosity and a desire to understand, we do more harm than good. All three aspects of our nature, united and in harmony, constitute the whole Man. There is a place to understand how spirit, soul, and body are different; but, through this understanding, we ought to see how they work together in harmony, and reflect the image of God.

The tri-partite nature of Man is as mysterious, or at least as complex, as any discussion of the Trinity. Man is a mystery as to his makeup and design because he was created in the image of God, the greatest mystery of all. One might as easily boast that he understands everything about the nature of God as boast that he understands everything about the nature of Man. We are all students here, ready and willing to learn, but thankfully we may also stand confident on what is clearly revealed.

The Scriptures consistently describe man as a three part being. The whole Man is made up of spirit, soul and body, (1 Thessalonians 5:23). God is a Spirit, and we fellowship with God through the spirit, and not the soul, nor the body.

A clear and simple illustration has become well known: with our bodies we contact the physical realm, and with our soul — our mind, will, and emotions — we contact the intellectual realm, and with our spirits we contact the spiritual realm. We commune with God and we worship God in our spirit. We renew our mind by meditation on the Word (Romans 12:2), deepening our understanding, and utilizing our intellectual faculties to the utmost. We keep our physical body under disciplined control.

From a close examination of Romans 8, we learn that the mind can be aligned with, or controlled, by the spirit; or the mind can be aligned with the physical body. These relationships or positions can change which further illustrates the difference between spirit, soul (mind) and body. This harmony, or disharmony, results in either life or death. Clearly, to Paul, an understanding of Man's tripartite nature is a life and death matter.

We see that true fellowship with God is between His Spirit and our spirit. After all, one can intellectually know much about God without having intimate fellowship with Him personally. Many have an understanding of the Bible, know about doctrines and God's attributes, but live in sin and are separated from God. That separation is spiritual. In this case, their intellect profits them nothing.

As you need physical food to nourish the physical body, and intellectual food to feed the mind, you need spiritual food to nourish your spirit. It's important to recognize the difference between an intellectual understanding of the Bible and a spiritual fellowship with a living Savior. When we receive the Word of God, we partake of "spirit and life" which doesn't happen when we read history, or science, or poetry. Many people read the Bible for the history, or science or poetry on a purely intellectual level, and fail to assimilate the "spirit and life" of a living God who is always speaking.

God heals through His Word by first healing the spirit of Man. Remember, sickness is first spiritual (death entered the world by sin) so also healing is first spiritual, then the mind is renewed, and then the body is healed. The Bible reads, "He sent His Word and *it* healed them…" (Psalms 107:20, Fenton translation).

Healing begins in the spirit when you receive the Word of God. It is life to your spirit. It renews the mind. It brings health to your body. This is the proper harmony of the whole man operating as spirit, soul, and body.

Proverbs 4:20-23
20 My son, attend to my words;
Incline thine ear unto my sayings.
21 Let them not depart from thine eyes;
Keep them in the midst of thine heart.
22 For they are life unto those that find them,
And health to all their flesh.
23 Keep thy heart with all diligence;
For out of it are the issues of life.

Jesus said the Word is life, and when you receive it in the heart, or spirit, it becomes health to all your flesh. It flows through the spirit and through the mind to the body. The soul of man must come under the dominion of the spirit and submit to the living Word of God. The body then walks in resurrection life when we "live according to the spirit," (Romans 8:5-11).

God desires for all to prosper and be in health according to how our soul prospers, (3 John 2). To say it another way, until your soul prospers what God desires for you will be delayed, or hindered in your life. God's will for you to prosper and be healthy is dependent on your soul prospering. God's express will, what God desires, should equal the state of your soul. There are times when your mind, your will, and your emotions are the very problems that must be resolved before you can receive the power and blessing of God. There are times when our mind is our enemy, our emotions are out of control and our will is weak and lacks discipline.

This is often the case when a person comes to the Lord

for the first time. They have lived a life of sin, but when they come to the altar that specific sin may not be the only problem: the state of their soul is the greater problem. Their mind tells them they are not worthy of His grace, their emotions explode with feelings of shame and condemnation, their will crumbles in despair without hope. Their soul is not prosperous.

But they heard God's Word preached, and that Word is "spirit and life." God's eternal Word imparts life to the eternal nature of Man. There is something in them at that moment that is greater than reasoning, more influential than emotion, and stronger than their will. That living Word received in their spirit, perhaps from one sermon preached, confronts the opposition of the soul, contradicts the false reasoning of the mind, overcomes the shame and guilt of emotion, and drives out all despair, bringing peace. It is not mental, or emotional, it is spiritual. You cannot think your way to heaven. Salvation is not a conversion of the mind, it is a new birth of the spirit. Man is born again. Then, and only then, the soul may begin to prosper.

This is why, in the plan of God, the spirit has dominion over the soul, and thereby the whole body.

Look at Galatians 5:16 — "This I say then, Walk in the Spirit, and ye shall not fulfil the lust of the flesh." Many people read this verse who suffer from spiritual dyslexia. They interpret it to mean exactly the opposite of what it says. It doesn't say, be free from sin and you will then walk in the spirit. It doesn't say, arrive at some level of holiness and you will be able to walk in the spirit. It clearly says, a walk in the spirit will not allow our fleshly body to fulfill its desires. Many try to develop spiritually by beginning with some denial of the flesh, or some education of the mind, hoping to arrive at some place where they can then be spiritual or walk in the spirit. This is not God's will or God's way and they approach it incorrectly for failure to understand the place of God's living Word in their spirit. We must FIRST walk in the spirit, then allow our spirit dominion over the soul, then allow our soul to rule over the body.

Do not forget Proverbs 3:5 — "Trust in the Lord with all thine heart; and lean not unto thine own understanding."

Do you see how the heart is placed in opposition to the understanding? We are not denigrating the intellect. We are not anti-intellectual. We seek to place the right priority where it belongs. We trust the heart first, then the head. The spirit should always have dominion over the soul. Do you see the order?

That which is received in the spirit rules over the mind. When the mind is renewed, our thinking transformed, we bring ourselves into line with His will and His ways. We begin to cooperate with the Kingdom of God and its principles in life.

The Centurion, whom Jesus described as having great faith, said, "speak the word only, and my servant shall be healed," (Matthew 8:8). He knew the power of God's Word to bring results. For him, it was the only thing required. His very thinking had come in line with how the Kingdom of God operates. His view of the words of Jesus was not concerning doctrine or content, but power and life. Jesus said, "My words are spirit and life," and so, the Centurion as much as said, "speak spirit and life and my servant shall be healed."

Let's return a moment to Proverbs 3:22, and consider the word "health." The Hebrew word originally meant *medicine*. God's word is medicine to all our flesh.

It is vitally important that we give the Word of God first priority in our life. When a doctor prescribes medicine for his patient, it is expected that the patient will purchase the medicine and follow the directions. If he doesn't follow the directions, but leaves the medicine lying unopened in his house, what good will be accomplished? How can the patient complain to the doctor if he hasn't even followed such simple instructions?

It is the same with God's Word. Why should we expect healing from God if we don't follow the simplest of instructions?

We are to attend to his words. We are to incline our ears to his sayings. We are not to allow them to depart from our eyes. We are told to keep them in our hearts.

Jesus said, "Take heed what ye hear: with what measure ye mete, it shall be measured to you: and unto you that hear shall more be given." (Mark 4:24).

On several occasions I have walked into hospital rooms to pray for the sick and found them watching the television, or reading romance books, or playing computer games. They were not taking God's Word as medicine, and many didn't even have a Bible. They wanted God to heal their bodies, but they had not placed God's Word as a priority in their life. They were paying thousands of dollars to the doctor but they were paying no attention to the Word of God.

I've seen how attending to God's Word, giving it the highest priority, can work as medicine in very powerful ways.

The Verse in Your Heart

The phone call came late at night. The woman on the other end was hysterical. It took me a moment to settle her down before I was able to understand what she was trying to tell me. "Charlie fell and they think his back is broken!" she was finally able to say. Her father-in-law was working with her husband at the construction site of their new house. They had been building it all summer. Charlie was working at the peak when he fell, passed through two levels and landed in the basement. He fell on his back across a board that was lying propped against the wall. The fall should have killed him.

I drove quickly to the hospital and entered the emergency room. Charlie's screams filled the hospital. One of the family rushed up to me and said, "They've taken a quick x-ray and his back is broken, but they need him to calm down to take more. The doctor has given him pain medication, and is waiting for it to take affect."

Together, Charlie's son and I walked into the room to pray for his father.

At first the doctor was angry to have us there. He barked "Stand in the hall, please, and let me do my job." I could see that he didn't have any consideration for the power of prayer. He didn't want us getting in his way with our "religious" beliefs.

Charlie continued screaming. He was completely out of control and hysterical from the intense pain. As the clock ticked on and on it became apparent that the medicine was not working. Charlie's screams made every second feel like an hour.

Eventually, the doctor came out, and walked to where Charlie's family and I had gathered. "I've given him three shots of pain medication," he said to us, "and by now he should be settling down." But there was a questioning look on his face. He turned around quickly as another horrible scream filled the hall. It made us all feel something of the agony that Charlie was enduring in the next room.

"We have to wait for him to settle down before we can get the x-ray's that we need," he said. I could see the worry on his face. He was trying to be very professional, but even he had his limits.

"If all you can do is wait," I said, "then it's our turn. Let me pray!" And without waiting for his answer, I brushed past him and walked into the room. He followed me and stood in the corner watching.

Charlie was lying on a hospital bed in the center of the room. His face was completely red and bathed in sweat. His eyes were clenched, and his mouth wide open and with every breath he screamed and screamed in pain. As I walked up to the bed, it seemed as though I could feel the pain radiating off of his body.

I knew his family was behind me praying, and it gave me more confidence. I knew I had to act boldly and with authority.

I placed my hands on each side of his head, and shouting at him I said, "Charlie, look at me!" I leaned over until we were face to face. I had to shout it again, "Charlie, look at me!" and he opened his eyes.

"Look in my eyes, Charlie!" I said. "Look me in the eyes!" I knew that through his pain there was only a faint glimmer of recognition in his mind. I wasn't sure he knew who I was, and I'm sure he didn't know where he was.

"Charlie," I shouted at him again. "We need to agree on a Scripture! Give me a verse, Charlie. Give me the verse that's in your heart right now!"

I don't really know why I asked him that. The Lord had led me to do it. I have since learned more how the Spirit of God operates. I know that God deals with our heart, or our spirits, and not our minds or our intellect. I know that in a time of trouble, the Spirit of God will bring Scripture to us to consider, to meditate on, to believe. The Holy Spirit has been sent into the earth to "teach us all things, and to bring all things into our remembrance," (John 14:26).

Charlie screamed again writhing in pain. Then his eyes locked on mine and with great effort, he opened his mouth and I heard him say, "The Lord is ..."

And I knew what he wanted to say! Holding his face in my hands I looked in his eyes and I finished his sentence for him. "My shepherd!"

His eyes widened, and I saw just a flicker of a fight deep inside him. "The Lord is my shepherd!" I shouted at him again, and this time I saw his lips moving in unison with mine. "Again, Charlie," I said. "Say it again!" and the third time we quoted it together.

I began quoting Psalm 23 out loud, shouting every word while Charlie followed me as best he could.

Psalm 23:1-6
1 The LORD is my shepherd; I shall not want.
2 He maketh me to lie down in green pastures: he leadeth me beside the still waters.

3 He restoreth my soul: he leadeth me in the paths of righteousness for his name's sake.

4 Yea, though I walk through the valley of the shadow of death, I will fear no evil: for thou art with me; thy rod and thy staff they comfort me.

5 Thou preparest a table before me in the presence of mine enemies: thou anointest my head with oil; my cup runneth over.

6 Surely goodness and mercy shall follow me all the days of my life: and I will dwell in the house of the LORD for ever.

As we finished quoting it the first time, I could see that he was beginning to regain control. The pain was still very present, and his body trembling, but there was a growing sense of clarity and confidence in his eyes.

We quoted it again, and then again the third time. This final time I sensed the pain receding.

I straightened up, and as I did I noticed the doctor approaching the bed. "The medicine is taking effect," he said. He didn't like the fact that I was touching Charlie. I knew he wanted me out of there and away from his patient.

What medicine? I thought. This is the medicine of God's Word!

I moved back a few steps when suddenly Charlie screamed again. I can't describe the pain, the fear, the terror in that scream. As quickly as you can snap your fingers, the same intensity of pain struck Charlie again, making him twist and jerk on the bed.

The doctor stepped back, and I stepped forward.

I took his face in my hands and once again lowered

myself to look into his eyes. With a voice of command and authority I began quoting the Lord's Psalm again and again. Like a drowning man reaching for a rope, Charlie joined me, mouthing the words, gasping desperately for breath and a release from this pain.

Once again, the peace of God settled on his body and filled the room. The power of God ran through him. I felt the anointing flowing from my hands into his body and driving the pain away. He began to breathe more easily, and began to speak more confidently, and louder.

"The Lord is my shepherd," we said together and he looked in my eyes with complete calm. We quoted it several times together until his breathing was calm and he settled down peacefully.

I looked up and saw the doctor approach. I knew they needed those x-rays, so I stepped back away from the bed. This time, with my eyes on Charlie, I watched the pain return. It hit him with physical force. He screamed. His body jerked. The pain had returned with intensity.

This third time I repeated ministering to Charlie with the doctor standing by the bed. It was obvious that it was not the medicine removing the pain, but the power of God's Word. The power of Jesus Christ was present in that room, and God's healing power was at work.

For the third time the pain left Charlie, and that time it did not return. I saw in the doctor's eyes a different look, perhaps one of respect. He had witnessed something he had never seen before.

They took Charlie from the room and additional x-rays were taken. I stayed for some time, ministering and praying with the family. They were people who knew how to pray! We were all confident that God had healed Charlie and that the reports would be good.

In the morning, a specialist came and examined the x-rays. The second set was not the same as the first. Charlie's back was not broken. The doctors were amazed and he went home the following day.

"My son, attend to my words; incline thine ear unto my sayings. Let them not depart from thine eyes; keep them in the midst of thine heart. For they are life unto those that find them, and health (or, medicine) to all their flesh." (Proverbs 4:20-23).

9

Learning to Live Free

There is no wavering in faith. It must be sure and steadfast. Before you can pray the prayer of faith and receive your healing from the Lord, you must be free from worry and fear.

Sickness and disease are terrible and devastating. Many have been given a sentence of death by their doctor and have lost all hope. After multiple operations there has been no change. They have spent their money on medicines that bring no cure. Death stands at the door. Pain has become their constant companion. Soon they are living with an enemy far worse than the sickness. Fear has found its home in them.

Fear and worry are the opposites of faith and meditation. Fear is faith in reverse. Fear is confidence that evil will come. Worry is a snare that holds our mind slave to negative thinking, overwhelmed with care and concern. We catch ourselves thinking thoughts that we should not think, brush them aside, and moments later they return again. Our thought life is under attack. Fear has found its place in us.

The Word of God is like a seed planted in the ground. The quality of the soil determines the harvest. Jesus said that a man's heart is the ground. Jesus taught that care or worry hinders the Word of God from taking root and growing in the heart, (Mark 4:19). It's impossible to worry and exercise faith at the same time.

We must see the importance of living free from worry. We must learn the secret of "taking every thought captive to the obedience of Christ," (2 Corinthians 10:5) until our minds are renewed on the principles of the Word of God.

Few Christians realize that the way they think determines their life. The Bible says, "As a man thinks in his heart, so is he," (Proverbs 23:7).

Free From Worry

Have you read how the storm came to destroy Jesus and His disciples?

They were crossing the sea when the storm arose and soon the boat was filled with water. Peter was a fisherman and had lived his life in boats and on the water. He knew his business on the sea. During this time of crisis, Peter couldn't understand how Jesus remained free from worry.

Notice how he asks, "Master, carest thou not that we perish?"

Mark 4:35-41

35 And the same day, when the even was come, he saith unto them, Let us pass over unto the other side.

36 And when they had sent away the multitude, they took him even as he was in the ship. And there were also with him other little ships.

37 And there arose a great storm of wind, and the waves beat into the ship, so that it was now full.

38 And he was in the hinder part of the ship, asleep on a pillow: and they awake him, and say unto him, Master, carest thou not that we perish?

39 And he arose, and rebuked the wind, and said unto the sea, Peace, be still. And the wind ceased, and there was a great calm.

40 And he said unto them, Why are ye so fearful? how is it that ye have no faith?

41 And they feared exceedingly, and said one to another, What manner of man is this, that even the wind and the sea obey him?

Did you notice that Jesus spoke what He desired? God does nothing without saying it first. Look at verse thirty five again. Jesus said, "Let us pass over unto the other side." Jesus didn't speak this for the benefit of His disciples alone. What He spoke He expected to come to pass.

Learn to use words like tools. Words accomplish things. Jesus used His words with purpose. On one occasion, Jesus spoke to a dead body, "Young man, I say unto you, arise!" (Luke 7:14). Notice that exactly. Jesus said, "I say unto you…" He spoke to a corpse. Jesus knew the power of His words, and He used them to produce results. He spoke to the dead and the dead lived.

Jesus went to sleep in the boat fully expecting to arrive on the other side. He taught His disciples to put faith in every word they spoke, just as He put faith in His own words, (Mark 11:23,24). But then the storm came. It beat on the ship until it was filled with water, and still Jesus slept on. He slept because He believed they would pass over to the other side. But Peter woke Him, saying "Don't you care what's happening?"

What was happening? There was a storm trying to destroy their lives, but there was another storm trying to steal their faith. Jesus could not afford to care. He could not afford the luxury of entering into worry or fear. Faith will not work in a fear-filled heart.

Jesus arose and rebuked the wind and the waves. He spoke to the problem, and it was calm. They stood in amazement looking at a man who could stop the wind and the waves. During the storm, Jesus had kept the peace and the calm in the midst of His heart. He had refused to enter into care, or worry, or fear. He never wavered.

Then Jesus asked them two questions: why are you filled with fear? And why are you without faith? Remember, faith will not work in a fear-filled heart.

Consider this with me. Do you really believe that "God shall supply all your need" (Philippians 4:19) when you spend the night tossing and turning in your bed for fear the money will not come? Have you honestly considered God's Word as the final authority when your mind is filled with worry and oppressive thoughts?

If Jesus had acted like Peter where would His faith have been?

You have prayed for healing but you are tossed to and fro on waves of fear and worry. Your mind turns from faith to fear and back again. You are unsettled and lack confidence that healing belongs to you. You wonder where the answer will come from. You are searching, but you never seem to find.

James said that when we pray the prayer of faith it should be without wavering:

James 1:6-8
6 But let him ask in faith, nothing wavering. For he that wavereth is like a wave of the sea driven with the wind and tossed.
7 For let not that man think that he shall receive any thing of the Lord.
8 A double minded man is unstable in all his ways.

How can we say we are standing firm in faith when worry and fear has filled our minds? Many have said, "I prayed in faith and nothing happened" and all the while fear was in their heart. While they prayed they wondered if the healing would come, they were worried that they would not receive. Maybe this time it will happen, they thought. A few days pass, and then they say "It must not be the will of God."

I remember hearing Oral Roberts preach years ago,

> *"Faith is not making yourself believe.
> Faith is when you cannot be made to doubt."*

Real faith never wavers, but actually grows stronger in the face of apparent denial. When troubles increase, so the peace of God increases. Our faith is based on God's Word, not on what we see or feel to the contrary.

Faith that wavers is guaranteed failure.

As long as there is a struggle to exercise unwavering faith, we must recognize that there are areas which need to be dealt with, attitudes that need to be changed or adjusted, and a resolve that needs to be developed in the integrity of God's Word.

Andrew Murray said,

> *"It is far easier for the flesh to submit without the answer to prayer than to yield itself to be searched and purified by the Spirit, until we have learned to pray the prayer of faith."*

We need to be honest with ourselves and be ready to change as we are instructed by the Lord. James said "let not that man think that he shall receive any thing of the Lord."

It's not a bad thing to discover the truth. When we are going in the wrong direction we should rejoice when someone shows us the correct way. When we are serious to find the answer we will be quick to embrace the truth.

You can live free from worry and fear. You can believe God with a perfect faith that never wavers. You can have peace in your heart when the storms of life have surrounded you. When it looks like all is lost and the end has come, you can stand and rebuke the wind and the waves.

The Psalmist says this about the man who puts God's Word first place in his life: "He shall not be afraid of evil tidings: his heart is fixed, trusting in the Lord. His heart is established," (Psalms 112:7,8).

When you are established in the Word of God you can speak to the disease and it will leave your body. You can rise up in faith that knows perfect peace and never wavers.

If we are honest with what we see in the Bible, we must admit that Jesus expected his disciples to do the same thing he had done. We are commanded to walk in His footsteps. They were amazed at his faith but He was amazed at their fear and unbelief. "How is it you have no faith?" He asked.

You can calm the storm of fear and worry in your life and exercise faith in a pure heart. Learn to cast your care on the Lord and live in the peace of God that goes far beyond your natural understanding.

Remember that God loves you and cares about you deeply. Later in life, Peter said, Cast "all your care upon him; for he careth for you," (1 Peter 5:7).

Peter learned this lesson well. Think of it! The man who asked the Savior, "Don't you care what is happening?" now says to us, "Cast your cares on Him!"

I can almost hear Peter say, "He has not left you alone.

He is there watching over you. Don't be afraid! He loves you so much!"

The first step of faith we take is to cast our cares into His hands and commit them to Him. "Commit thy way unto the LORD; trust also in him; and he shall bring it to pass," (Psalms 37:5).

He is a faithful Father. His love is the greatest reason to live free from worry and fear. We can take our troubles, our worries, our concerns, our heart aches and sorrows, and lay them all at His feet. He will take them every one.

How many times fear and worry have come to my mind! I thank God for His precious promises. In the middle of the night, I have risen from the bed and knelt before Him. I've lifted my hands to worship Him. I have thanked Him for His love and His mercy. I have praised Him for not forsaking me, for not leaving me alone.

"Father," I have prayed. "I know you love me. I'm so thankful for your love. Right now I am attacked by these thoughts of fear and worry. But I know you love me, I know you care about me. I'm turning them all over to you. I'm placing them in your hands. I commit my life and my future and my health to you. I love you so much, Father."

And then I worship Him freely and honestly from my heart. I find myself thinking thoughts about Him and His love instead of thoughts about my problems and my needs.

Fear will not go by resisting the thought. Worry will not disappear by trying to clear your mind. To free your mind from fear and worry you have to do more than refuse to think the thoughts, you must replace the thoughts. Fill your mind with new thoughts and the old must leave.

Replace the thought with a more powerful thought.

God will keep you in perfect peace when your mind is fixed and focused on Him, (Isaiah 26:3). You have a choice to think thoughts of fear or thoughts of faith. Boldly take Him at His Word. Cast your care on Him and fill your thoughts with the Word of God.

If necessary, speak the Word out loud in your room. Dominate your mind by speaking God's Word loudly until your thoughts are filled with the truth that you confess. When worry tries to enter your mind, take the Sword of the Spirit and fight back. Speak God's Word constantly.

It is a fight. Paul called it a fight of faith, (1 Timothy 6:12). We have been given weapons for this warfare, and they are mighty through God to deliver. These weapons pull down Satan's stronghold that has been set up in your mind. They tear down the imaginations that are against you in your thought life. They bring the thoughts of your mind captive to the truth that is in Jesus.

> **2 Corinthians 10:3-6**
> 3 For though we walk in the flesh, we do not war after the flesh:
> 4 (For the weapons of our warfare are not carnal, but mighty through God to the pulling down of strong holds;)
> 5 Casting down imaginations, and every high thing that exalteth itself against the knowledge of God, and bringing into captivity every thought to the obedience of Christ.

The Sword of the Spirit is a spiritual weapon when we

speak the Word of God on lips of faith. When Jesus faced Satan in the wilderness He showed us how to use this powerful weapon. At every attack, and in the face of every temptation, Jesus said, "It is written…"

Learn to speak the Word of God until your mind is quiet on the promises that God has made to you. See yourself the way God has said it. At one time you saw yourself defeated, but now learn to see what the Word of God says! You "are more than a conqueror through Christ who loves you!" (Romans 8:37).

You cannot think defeat when you are speaking victory. You cannot think failure when you are speaking God's Word. "Thanks be to God, which giveth us the victory through our Lord Jesus Christ," (1 Corinthians 15:57).

Learn to fill your mind with thoughts that build you up and give you hope. Become diligent to consider what your mind dwells upon. You are careful to observe what you eat and conscious to stay healthy through a good diet. Learn to diet your mind on God's Word and stop thinking thoughts that tear you down.

Look where Paul said,

> **Philippians 4:6-8**
>
> 6 Be careful for nothing; but in every thing by prayer and supplication with thanksgiving let your requests be made known unto God.
>
> 7 And the peace of God, which passeth all understanding, shall keep your hearts and minds through Christ Jesus.
>
> 8 Finally, brethren, whatsoever things are true, whatsoever things are honest, whatsoever things

are just, whatsoever things are pure, whatsoever things are lovely, whatsoever things are of good report; if there be any virtue, and if there be any praise, think on these things.

Paul is very specific, giving us instruction on what thoughts to allow in our mind. In some ways his instructions work like a filter. Something you think about may qualify in one way, but does it qualify in all? Many bad experiences are true, but do they meet the other qualifications?

Examine what you are thinking. First, is it true? and then even further, is it honest? Is it just? Is it pure? Be sure that what you are thinking about is lovely, and be discriminating. Is it a good report? Does it possess virtue? Is it worthy of praise? These are the things to think on.

Have you considered that you are a result of what you have been thinking?

Everywhere I go I find people who are insecure and who lack confidence. From the outside, it appears that they are humble and submissive to authority. They give the appearance of harmony and peace, but inside they have no peace and no victory. They are so insecure they are looking for someone to tell them what to do. They are not confident in making decisions. They would rather have someone else make the decisions for them. They tell themselves that they are followers, but in fact they are defeated leaders.

These inadequacies exist in people because of a life long pattern of thought. They have become what they have allowed themselves to think. "As a man thinks in his heart, so is he," (Proverbs 23:7).

It's not what happens to you that makes you who you are, it's how you respond; it's what you do when things happen to you that determines who you are.

As a young teenager, I came to Jesus at the point of suicide. Circumstances drove me to despair. I lived for nearly a year considering death every day. Many times I went so far as to place the barrel of a gun in my mouth. It was only the grace of God, and the prayers of my mother, that kept me from pulling the trigger.

It's not important to describe my life, or what I experienced, but I think it might be helpful to share with you some of the steps that God showed me that brought victory out of defeat. These same steps will help you appropriate the Word of God into your life, change the way that you think, and transform your life into what God has originally intended.

I was born again and had received Jesus as the Lord of my life, but I was still living a life filled with despair and depression. I had been changed in my spirit, in the heart, but my mind was still filled with the same pattern of thoughts from the past. I had not let go of the old way of thinking.

We are not walking in God's best until we put off the old way of life, the life we lived without Christ, and put on the new life in Christ Jesus. Paul said, "put on the new man, which is renewed in knowledge after the image of him that created him," (Colossians 3:10).

The knowledge of who you are in Christ will renew your life. The renewing of the mind brings transformation,

(Romans 12:2). We must begin to think according to what God has done in us, and allow the truth of that redemption to dominate our thoughts. This knowledge from the Word of God is "after the image of him that created him" or, in other words, this is the knowledge of how God originally intended you to be. We were created in His image. Sin entered and destroyed that image. Through the renewing of our minds, and thinking Scripturally, we renew ourselves into the image that God intended. Only then can we experience the perfect will of God.

The first step that God showed me was the simple fact that my thinking was wrong. I remember awakening very early one morning. I had not had a peaceful night's sleep for months. My mind was tormenting me and I could not find any peace. At times, it seemed like a motor was running in my head. Constantly, I was fighting depressive thoughts, but they would not go away. I didn't know how to make them go away, and little by little I was accepting them. It was driving me to suicide.

I sat on the edge of my bed weeping, holding my head in my hands when God revealed the simple truth to me: I am not thinking accurately. This isn't right. If I keep this up, I am going to die. Eventually, I will pull the trigger.

I had always been proud of my intelligence. My teachers had always praised me for having a sharp mind. They had sent me to special schools saying I had great promise. For the first time in my life, I realized that I couldn't trust my own thoughts. I wasn't thinking correctly. I couldn't trust my mind.

Then I saw the second great truth that changed me

forever. I picked up a Bible and held it before me. I said it out loud in the room, "If I can think these thoughts, from these pages, then I can trust those thoughts."

I didn't know that what God had showed me was exactly what Paul had said about spiritual warfare. We walk in the flesh, but our fight is not with the flesh. You cannot bring a supernatural change by using natural methods. It takes supernatural methods.

As my wife Teri told me years later, "Spiritual problems require spiritual solutions."

I was learning to bring "into captivity every thought to the obedience of Christ" (2 Corinthians 10:5) when I realized that I needed to think God's thoughts, and not my own.

The weapons of spiritual warfare are truth, righteousness, the power of the gospel, faith, salvation, the word of God, and prayer, (Ephesians 6:14-18).

By refusing to think thoughts according to the old pattern, and thinking only what I found in the Word of God, I was putting into practice a very powerful spiritual weapon. Satan had raised a stronghold in my mind, a pattern of thinking that was the source of all my problems. The sword of the Spirit is the Word of God, and I had discovered its secret.

It took some time before I learned the third truth. You control what you are thinking by the words of your mouth. You have to think what you are speaking, therefore you can control what you think by controlling what you say. In other words, if you constantly speak God's word you will have to constantly think God's word. By giving voice to God's word, you give it dominion in your heart and in your mind. The more you speak the words of the Bible, the more they will become established in your mind.

We read in the Psalms, "Set a watch, O LORD, before my mouth; keep the door of my lips," (141:3). David knew that it was important to watch what he spoke, as faith is released by our words; but also, he recognized that what goes on in the heart, the thoughts we think in our minds, have as great an impact upon us. "Let the words of my mouth, and the meditation of my heart, be acceptable in thy sight, O LORD, my strength, and my redeemer," (Psalms 19:14)

Meditation is a principle that changes the way you think, and more. Meditation is the channel from the head to the heart. In the original Hebrew, the word meditation means *to mutter*. There is no meditation, in the Hebrew mind, without speaking, or muttering. As we find in Psalm 32:30, "the mouth of the righteous shall meditate wisdom." This vocal law controls the activity of the mind.

Joshua 1:8

8 This book of the law shall not depart out of thy mouth; but thou shalt meditate therein day and night, that thou mayest observe to do according to all that is written therein: for then thou shalt make thy way prosperous, and then thou shalt have good success.

God told Joshua that the "book of the law" should not depart out of his mouth, or he should constantly be speaking God's Word. Day and night his meditation was to rest on the word of God. Meditation, or muttering

God's word is the first step to becoming preoccupied with God's truth, and destroying the effects of thinking contrary to God's will.

There is a point where you will have to force yourself to become preoccupied on the things of God. This is spiritual warfare, and in many cases the patterns of thought that have dominated your mind have been established over years and years. It will take some time, but not a long time, for you to break those patterns of thought by thinking in line with God's word.

In the past, I was preoccupied with thoughts of despair, grief and discouragement. As soon as I would awake, negative thoughts would flood into my mind. Now I was learning to become filled with the word of God, dominated by its thoughts, and preoccupied with its truth.

What a difference it makes to awake and the thoughts of God's Word fill your mind!

The Bible tells us that when we fill our minds with the Word of God it will dominate our consciousness and our thinking, it will rise up in our minds when we awake. "When thou goest, it shall lead thee; when thou sleepest, it shall keep thee; and when thou awakest, it shall talk with thee. For the commandment is a lamp; and the law is light; and reproofs of instruction are the way of life," (Proverbs 6:22,23).

10

Presumption is not Faith

It is one thing to talk about God healing the sick but quite another thing to talk about God healing you. What a wonderful day when you realize that God's Word applies to you personally. His promises were made to you, and He is faithful to do everything He has said He would do.

Jesus said, "If ye continue in my word, then are ye my disciples indeed; And ye shall know the truth, and the truth shall make you free," (John 8:31,32). The truth alone cannot make you free. It's knowing the truth that really counts. It's knowing God's will for your life and continuing in it.

The Word is alive, (Hebrews 4:16). It is a living thing. You can only come to know someone by spending time with them, and it is the same with God and His Word. We come to know the Father by spending time fellowshipping with Him in the Word. His Word is a revelation of His heart.

We cooperate with the living Word and base our life on God's promises. We are walking with Him. Together, through the Spirit and through the Word, He has a part in our daily affairs. We are working together with Him. We receive His living promises as we read the Bible, and breathe them back to Him in prayer.

When problems arise, the first thing in our mind is the question "What does God's Word have to say about this?"

Prayer becomes a powerful force in our walk. When we see a need, we respond in prayer. When we encounter a sorrowing friend, we take up their burden in our prayers. We turn every need into an opportunity to commune with the One who meets every need. We learn to respond to life by consulting with Him. We are His voice of authority in the earth. When we speak His Word we enforce His will. We are His body, His hands, His feet. The Holy Spirit has entered into the ministry of intercession with us, (Romans 8:26,27). Together we pray the perfect prayer and the will of God is established.

When we approach a difficulty that seems too much for us, we quietly remember that "He is the strength of our life," (Psalms 73:26). We remind ourselves that we "can do all things through Christ who strengthens" us, (Philippians 4:13).

If it doesn't look like we will have the money to meet a pressing need, the promises rise up in our heart. We know that above all else, God "desires us to prosper and be in health," (3 John 2).

His Word is on our lips, and we find ourselves quoting

from the Psalms, "Praise ye the Lord! Blessed is the man that feareth the Lord, that delighteth greatly in his commandments... Wealth and riches shall be in his house: and his righteousness endureth for ever," (Psalms 112:1-3).

Time after time we encounter difficulties, trials, problems, discouragements, and setbacks. Time after time we see the faithful hand of God, and realize that while "Many are the afflictions of the righteous, the Lord delivers them out of them ALL," (Psalms 34:19).

We stand firm in our faith. We refuse to worry, "but by prayer and supplication, and with a heart of thanksgiving, we make our requests known to God," (Philippians 4:6).

Walking on the Word

Matthew 14:23-31
23 And when he had sent the multitudes away, he went up into a mountain apart to pray: and when the evening was come, he was there alone.
24 But the ship was now in the midst of the sea, tossed with waves: for the wind was contrary.
25 And in the fourth watch of the night Jesus went unto them, walking on the sea.
26 And when the disciples saw him walking on the sea, they were troubled, saying, It is a spirit; and they cried out for fear.
27 But straightway Jesus spake unto them, saying, Be of good cheer; it is I; be not afraid.
28 And Peter answered him and said, Lord, if it be thou, bid me come unto thee on the water.

> 29 And he said, Come. And when Peter was come down out of the ship, he walked on the water, to go to Jesus.
> 30 But when he saw the wind boisterous, he was afraid; and beginning to sink, he cried, saying, Lord, save me.
> 31 And immediately Jesus stretched forth his hand, and caught him, and said unto him, O thou of little faith, wherefore didst thou doubt?

Peter desired to be like Christ. Later in life Peter wrote that Christ was our example, (1 Peter 2:21) and that we are to follow in his footsteps. Perhaps Peter was mindful of the lessons he learned when he followed Jesus' footsteps and walked on the water.

Peter was so bold when he said, "Lord, if it is really you, tell me to come to you on the water!" Jesus said to him, "Come!"

Jesus spoke to Peter, personally. Remember, only Peter left the boat. The other Disciples stayed behind. Why? Jesus didn't speak to them, and they had no Scripture nor Biblical promise to stand on.

Some people want to walk on the water like Peter, but has God spoken to them? If there is no specific promise in the Bible then where is the basis for their faith? Jesus told Peter to walk on the water, and Peter believed the personal word he had received. Jesus said, "Come!"

If we have no clear revelation of His will, no promise to claim, then we have no basis for faith. Faith begins where the will of God is known. You should not try to rise from your sick bed because someone else did the same. This is presumption and not faith. Your faith is based on His Word, not on testimonies, or experiences, emotions, or feelings.

Faith comes by hearing and hearing by the word of God, (Romans 10:17) and sometimes God speaks to us personally, as He did Peter, but all the time the Scriptures speak to us. Keep this in mind. You don't need a personal word from the Lord, or from the Spirit, when you have a clear promise from the Scripture!

Some years ago I met a man who had recently repented of his sins and was saved. He had lived a life of sin and his wife had left him. Due to his former lifestyle her actions were very understandable. The loneliness and the loss made him ask questions he had failed to ask before: about life, about purpose, and about God. He recognized his sin and made Jesus the Lord of his life.

He told me how God had spoken to him soon after he was born again. God said that his wife would return to him. This became an area of constant prayer, and for months he tried to be reconciled to his wife. It seemed the harder he tried, the worse their relationship became. It was a terrible time for him emotionally, and his Christian walk was not very stable. Eventually, he became depressed and attempted suicide. Only God's grace saved him.

One day we were talking about his problems, about his wife, and about what he believed God had spoken to him. It startled me when I saw the truth, but the Holy Spirit impressed it on me very clearly.

I said to him, "God never spoke to you that your wife would return!"

"What?" he demanded. I could see that it made him angry.

"God never told you that your wife was going to come back to you!" I repeated. The Holy Spirit had made it all so very plain to me.

"How can you say that?" he asked. He had spent so much time trying to be reconciled to her, but it only caused him further pain.

"I can guarantee that God never spoke to you about it," I said. "If God had spoken to you then you would have faith to believe it. But all these months that I have known you I haven't seen any faith in that direction. Not even one time! You don't believe she is coming back, in fact the very issue has been used by the devil and he has nearly killed you!"

I could see that he didn't quite understand what I was trying to say.

"Faith comes by hearing the Word, and you have no faith. I don't believe God ever spoke a word to you about it, or you would have the faith to receive it."

Presumption Is Not Faith

Sometimes people do things because they think something is expected of them. They want to fit in. They have learned the right words to say and the right things to do in order to look like people of faith. They make a faith "mistake." This is presumption, and presumption is not faith.

One time a woman in our Church visited my wife and I. She asked if we would meet with her and her husband. She didn't know what to do, she said, and wanted our counsel. I could see concern written on her face.

We sat with them in their home, the husband at her side. Doctors had performed several medical tests, she told us. They had found cancer and they wanted to operate immediately. She told us all the facts very carefully, one by one. It was everything for her not to cry. My wife and I felt compassion as she opened up her heart and shared her fears, her questions, and her faith.

What Should She Do?

She had been hearing the Word of God preached on a weekly basis for over a year. Everything she had been taught from the Bible was new and exciting. She loved to hear the many personal testimonies from those who had been healed. Now she was faced with one of the greatest challenges of her life. Should she have the operation, as the doctors wanted; or, should she pray and believe God to be healed?

"I'm not sure if I have the faith to be healed," she said.

I was very interested in another statement she made. "I'm afraid of the operation. If I don't have the operation, is it faith or is it fear? How do I know if I have enough faith?"

My wife and I shared with her how we cannot afford to act on fear at any time. It wouldn't be right to avoid the operation, nor would it be right to have the operation, based on fear. You should never let fear hide behind a masquerade of faith. Presumption is a great enemy of faith. Some think that faith is simply acting and saying the right things like a magic formula. They see and hear what other people do and they copy what they see. That doesn't mean they are motivated by faith. Our faith must be based on the Word of God, not on the word of a man, on someone's testimony, or what we have seen happen in another person's life.

As encouraging as a testimony can be, it doesn't build faith. Faith comes by hearing the Word of God, (Romans 10:17), and without a firm foundation of faith all our words and actions will be empty of power and effectiveness.

Some people don't take medicine, or they refuse to see a doctor, because they think Christians shouldn't do these things. They are afraid that other people will think they are not spiritual. I've seen this happen in many churches that are strong on faith. But that's not faith, that is presumption.

Faith is not making yourself believe, faith is when you cannot be made to doubt. For example, when someone asks us, "Should I stop taking my medicine because I believe I am healed?" we usually answer them, "If you have to ask, then it would be better for you to keep taking the medicine!"

We told her that even if she went through the operation Jesus would be with her. We could pray that God would anoint the doctors hands, and that the operation would be a success.

"The important thing to realize is that fear has no right to exist in your life," we said. "This is a big decision, and an important decision. Only you can tell us what you believe. When you are confident that you know what you believe, then we can pray the prayer of agreement that Jesus taught in Matthew 18:19,20.

Presumption is not Faith

Matthew 18:19,20

19 Again I say unto you, That if two of you shall agree on earth as touching any thing that they shall ask, it shall be done for them of my Father which is in heaven.

20 For where two or three are gathered together in my name, there am I in the midst of them.

She went before the Lord and prayed for several days. Heart preparation is necessary and important before any operation! She fasted and ministered to the Lord in prayer and worship. When she returned, we asked her "Have you made a decision?"

"Yes," She answered, "I am not going to have the operation."

"And what made you decide that?" we asked.

She was quick to answer. "When I was praying, I simply asked myself, What do I believe?" There was a smile on her face and confidence in her voice. "You know what?" she said. "I believe Jesus Christ is my healer, and that He bore my sickness and disease on the Cross!"

"Pray for me," she added, "and I will receive my healing now!" Her words and her actions were motivated by the faith in her heart and she was healed.

When the doctors heard about her decision they were very upset. One claimed that I was a charlatan, the leader of a cult, and not a man of God. He couldn't believe that she would follow my advice and not his. His medical reports were proof that she needed this operation, and she needed to have it immediately before it was too late.

But her faith was not based on what I said, it was not

based on what my wife said, it was not based on what others have said. Her faith was based on the words of Jesus Christ, and as He said to the woman with the issue of blood, "Daughter, your faith has made you whole!" so it can be said of her. Later, the same doctor wrote a letter reporting that her body was completely free of cancer. Her faith had made her whole! At the time of this writing, more than thirty years later, she is still alive and rejoicing in Jesus!

The brother I mentioned earlier who was trying to be restored to his wife, had no faith in his heart because he had received no such promise from the Father. He had not heard the Lord speak in a special way, either, as Peter heard Jesus say "*Come!*" The other disciples were left sitting in the boat, and so was he.

In fact, concerning a similar situation the Bible clearly states "For what knowest thou, O wife, whether thou shalt save thy husband? or how knowest thou, O man, whether thou shalt save thy wife?" (1 Corinthians 7:16) Without any promise, the man could exercise no faith. His actions were based on presumption, and he never did receive.

All Things That Pertain To Life

Jesus told Peter, "*Come!*" and faith came into his heart that he could walk on the water. Actually, Peter never walked on the water, he walked on the integrity and authority of Jesus' words. His faith wasn't in the water's ability to hold him up, his faith was in Jesus' words.

We may not walk on the water but we can always walk on His Word. We have many Bible promises to base our faith on: specific promises God has given so we can partake of everything we need in our spiritual and natural lives.

2 Peter 1:3,4
> 3 According as his divine power hath given unto us all things that pertain unto life and godliness, through the knowledge of him that hath called us to glory and virtue:
> 4 Whereby are given unto us exceeding great and precious promises: that by these ye might be partakers of the divine nature, having escaped the corruption that is in the world through lust.

God's promises written in the Bible are as powerful as the words Jesus spoke to Peter when He said, "Come!" The promises in the Bible are as powerful as if Jesus stood before you in the flesh and spoke the very same thing! God's Word is alive! (Hebrews 4:16).

In fact, if Jesus were to appear to you what more would He say? What one thing would He say concerning your case that He has not already said?

He has already said, "I wish above all things that you may prosper and be in health even as your soul prospers," (3 John 2). Should He appear before you at this very instant, He would say exactly the same thing!

We can learn to walk on the integrity of God's Word by learning how Peter walked on the integrity of Jesus' words spoken to him personally. We must come to the place that we consider every Bible promise as spoken to us personally.

The Bible is God speaking to you!

Peter Walked On The Water

When considering this story, most people remember that Peter fell into the water. They focus on his failure. That's true, but don't forget one fact: Peter walked on the water. Even one step was a miracle, and Peter took more than one!

In the face of apparent victory – it was an incredible miracle that he could walk on the water – Peter began to look at the wind, and looking at the wind he became afraid.

Fear is often irrational and without foundation. What does wind have to do with someone walking on the water? Are we to believe that it's possible to walk on the water when there is no wind? If water is calm, can a man walk on it? Of course not!

Remember the woman who was healed of cancer? The doctor's reports were like the wind and the waves. If they were not dealt with they would bring fear, and she would not be able to receive. She had to decide whose report she would believe, the doctors or the report of the Lord?

> **Isaiah 53:1-5**
> 1 Who hath believed our report? and to whom is the arm of the LORD revealed?
> 2 For he shall grow up before him as a tender plant, and as a root out of a dry ground: he hath no form nor comeliness; and when we shall see him, there is no beauty that we should desire him.

> 3 He is despised and rejected of men; a man of sorrows, and acquainted with grief: and we hid as it were our faces from him; he was despised, and we esteemed him not.
> 4 Surely he hath borne our griefs, and carried our sorrows: yet we did esteem him stricken, smitten of God, and afflicted.
> 5 But he was wounded for our transgressions, he was bruised for our iniquities: the chastisement of our peace was upon him; and with his stripes we are healed.

She decided to believe the report of the Lord, and declared that "by his stripes I am healed!" The wind and the waves were very real to Peter. The Doctor's reports were factual and well documented. Neither hold any comparison to the miracle power of God.

But Peter began looking at the effects of the wind and stopped looking at the word of God. Fear entered into his heart, and we know that faith cannot operate in a heart filled with fear. Peter began to sink.

At the moment, Peter cried out, "Lord save me!" Jesus immediately stretched out his hand and lifted him up.

Jesus said to Peter, "You have little faith! Why did you doubt?"

Let's examine this for a moment. Exactly what did Peter doubt? Have you ever thought about that before?

Peter never lost faith in Jesus. He cried out, "Lord, save me!" and the Lord saved him. Here was a man sinking in the water being held up by another man standing on the water! Isn't that interesting? Peter doubted that he could walk on the water, but he believed that Jesus could both walk on the water AND HOLD HIM UP TOO!

So what was it Peter doubted? He doubted his own ability to walk on the water; or as we have recently learned, Peter doubted his ability to walk on the Word of God.

Many people believe that God heals – He heals other people. Many people believe that God answers prayer – other people's prayers. Many people believe that God works miracles – for other people. But God healing them, or answering their prayer, or working a miracle for them personally – that is another question.

They have no faith in their faith. Their faith has been stolen because they don't believe in their own ability to walk in faith. They live in a consciousness of their sin and failure.

Every spiritual failure can be traced to a sin consciousness. It destroys faith. It destroys spiritual initiative in the heart. It gives to man a spiritual inferiority complex. It makes man a spiritual hitchhiker. He is ever searching for someone who can pray the prayers he cannot pray himself. He doesn't believe in himself, or in his ability to stand before God. He doesn't believe in what Christ has done for him personally, or what he, in Christ, has become. He forgets that he has rights and privileges as a child of God. He is well acquainted with all his failure and inability. He rehearses them daily.

He lives according to his past, not according to his future that is in Christ. He is cleansed of his sin, forgiven of his past, but he does not walk in the light of what that means. If he did, nothing but praise would be on his lips.

> **Colossians 1:12-14**
> 12 Giving thanks unto the Father, which hath made us meet to be partakers of the inheritance of the saints in light:
> 13 Who hath delivered us from the power of darkness, and hath translated us into the kingdom of his dear Son:
> 14 In whom we have redemption through his blood, even the forgiveness of sins:

God has made us able to partake of our inheritance. He has given us the ability to receive. We have been delivered from the power of darkness, from Satan's dominion over our lives, and transported into the Kingdom of His love. We have this redemption now. It belongs to us.

It is a source of continual praise and thanksgiving, this knowledge that we can walk in His abundant provision and blessing.

Jesus commanded Paul to preach this Gospel and set people free, "To open their eyes, and to turn them from darkness to light, and from the power of Satan unto God, that they may receive forgiveness of sins, and inheritance among them which are sanctified by faith that is in me," (Acts 26:18).

God wants you to receive.

11

Established in Righteousness

At some point you have to have confidence in your own faith. It's time to stop being a spiritual hitchhiker, always depending on the faith of others, always asking others to do the labor of prayer on your behalf. Develop your own faith life and become that person whom people call on when they need a miracle, or a prayer answered, or a healing manifested.

You must become established in righteousness. "Being made righteous by faith, we have peace with God," (Romans 5:1). You live and walk knowing that you are at peace with God. You approach Him freely, confident in your standing and knowing that He hears you when you pray.

Righteousness is your right to approach God. You can

enter heaven's throne and transact prayer business with the Creator of the Universe. You are at peace with God and at home in His presence. You have the ability to stand in the presence of God without a sense of guilt, inferiority, shame or fear because you belong there. Righteousness enables you to come before God. Righteousness enables you to represent Him in the earth. Jesus performed what He came to do: He obtained redemption for Man, broke both the guilt and power of Sin, and restored fellowship back with the Father.

Now we must take our place as Sons and Daughters of God.

Ambassadors

An ambassador is defined as "*an officially delegated representative of a sovereign.*" We are ambassadors for Christ.

> **2 Corinthians 5:17 – 6:1**
>
> 17 Therefore if any man be in Christ, he is a new creature: old things are passed away; behold, all things are become new.
>
> 18 And all things are of God, who hath reconciled us to himself by Jesus Christ, and hath given to us the ministry of reconciliation;
>
> 19 To wit, that God was in Christ, reconciling the world unto himself, not imputing their trespasses unto them; and hath committed unto us the word of reconciliation.

> 20 Now then we are ambassadors for Christ, as though God did beseech you by us: we pray you in Christ's stead, be ye reconciled to God.
> 21 For he hath made him to be sin for us, who knew no sin; that we might be made the righteousness of God in him.
> 6:1 We then, as workers together with him, beseech you also that ye receive not the grace of God in vain.

Jesus, who knew no sin, was made to be sin for us that we, who knew no righteousness, might be made righteous. We are made righteous with His righteousness. We are accepted before God according to His merits, not our own.

The missionary and author Mrs. C. Nuzum wrote very well in her book *The Life of Faith* when she said,

> *"Just as Jesus chose what we were, so we must choose to be exactly what He is, and no more let go, or turn away than Jesus did. God is just as willing to let us have all that is in Jesus as He was to let Jesus have what was in us."*

The righteousness mentioned here (verse 21) is to qualify us as ambassadors; first, it is God in Christ reconciling the world to Himself, and now, it is God in us. It is God in us, just as present a reality as it was God in Christ, reconciling the world to Himself.

We are workers together with Him. God is beseeching lost men everywhere by us, and we stand in the place of Christ, that through us the same message and the same voice is heard: be reconciled to God!

Man was originally made in the image of God, so that when Jesus became a man, He was still in the image of God. Jesus is fully God, or as the early Church fathers often said, Jesus is very God. He is also fully man. He is the God Man. He is not half man and half God, but fully God and fully Man. He is the One where God and Man unite in total. Just as He is the fullness of the Godhead bodily, (Colossians 2:9) so He is also the fullness of Man and we find our completion in Him. He is the last Adam, come to earth a life-giving spirit, (1 Corinthians 15:45). He is the representative Man, the express image of God's person, (Hebrews 1:3). There is a Man seated at the right hand of God. It is in this union with Him, where we stand as members of His body, that is the fullness of Him who fills all things, (Ephesians 1:23).

Our union with Him is the end of condemnation, (Romans 8:1). Righteousness enables you to stop doubting yourself, hesitating over your own inabilities. We are one with the Father.

Lazarus had been dead for four days, but look how boldly Jesus told them to, "Roll away the stone!" Jesus was able to exercise unwavering faith in the presence of death and decay because of His righteousness before God. There was no hesitation or debate. He didn't wonder, what if God does not hear me? What if my prayer goes unanswered? What if Lazarus is still dead? He knew where He stood with God. He knew His Father always heard His prayer.

He knew that God was in Him reconciling the world to Himself. He was God's ambassador.

John 11:41-43

41 Then they took away the stone from the place where the dead was laid. And Jesus lifted up his eyes, and said, Father, I thank thee that thou hast heard me.

42 And I knew that thou hearest me always: but because of the people which stand by I said it, that they may believe that thou hast sent me.

43 And when he thus had spoken, he cried with a loud voice, Lazarus, come forth!

You cannot exercise real Bible faith until you have settled the issue of your personal standing before God. You must be settled in the fact that God loves and cares for you personally before you can exercise a faith that never wavers.

Have you considered that when you think thoughts that degrade you, thoughts of how unworthy you are, how sinful you are – have you considered that you are giving Satan the glory in your life, magnifying his victories over God's? When you give place to these feelings and attitudes you are looking at the wind and the waves, just like Peter. They have no power over the redemption that is in Christ Jesus.

Either His blood has cleansed you, or it has not. Either His love is for you, or it is not. Either He has made you a new creation in Christ, or He has not. How can you dare call yourself unworthy when Christ has cleansed you?

What He has done for you He wants to do in you, and those things He has done in you, He wants to do through you and bless all mankind.

You have to know what to say when faced with feelings of being unworthy or sinful. "What shall we then say to these things? If God be for us, who can be against us?" (Romans 8:31).

Do you know that God has given everything for you? If "He spared not his own Son, but delivered him up for us all, how shall he not with him also freely give us all things?" (Romans 8:32).

Do you know that your sins are forgiven and forgotten? Do you remember that He said, "For I will be merciful to their unrighteousness, and their sins and their iniquities will I remember no more," (Hebrews 8:12).

Do you realize that you stand "holy and without blame before him in love?" (Ephesians 1:4).

Why do you rehearse your failures, your sins, your problems when you could rehearse these great facts? The redemption that is in Christ Jesus is an accomplished fact.

What would your life be like if you abandoned yourself to these great truths? What would your life be like if you took Him at His Word? What would it mean to you if you stopped hanging on to doubt and unbelief, and refused to consider yourself unworthy or sinful anymore? What would happen if you based your life on the fact of Christ's great redemption? If you finally saw yourself as God sees you? What if you believed that you are who God says you are? What if you believed that God is who He says He is?

Then you would know, in the calm assurance of faith, that you can do what He says you can do. You would realize that you are more than a conqueror right now because He loves you, (Romans 8:37) and that sickness, poverty, fear and failure no longer belong in your life.

You would recognize that you are the victor now, not Satan, not sickness, not poverty, not fear. You would recognize that the dominion of Satan has ended, and the Lordship of Jesus Christ is effective in your life.

This is how your soul prospers, when God's will for you is received into your heart in the full assurance of faith, when you have confidence in your heart that the Father hears you in everything, just as He heard Jesus.

> **1 John 4:20-22**
> 20 For if our heart condemn us, God is greater than our heart, and knoweth all things.
> 21 Beloved, if our heart condemn us not, then have we confidence toward God.
> 22 And whatsoever we ask, we receive of him, because we keep his commandments, and do those things that are pleasing in his sight.

Remember, faith never begs, but demands by right of inheritance with praise and thanksgiving. You are learning what belongs to you, what your inheritance is, and what blessings are yours. You are learning to take your place. You are being "filled with the knowledge of his will in all wisdom and spiritual understanding that ye might walk worthy of the Lord, being fruitful in every good work, and increasing in the knowledge of God," (Colossians 1:9,10).

12

Enemies of Faith

Mark 6:2-6

2 And when the sabbath day was come, he began to teach in the synagogue: and many hearing him were astonished, saying, From whence hath this man these things? and what wisdom is this which is given unto him, that even such mighty works are wrought by his hands?

3 Is not this the carpenter, the son of Mary, the brother of James, and Joses, and of Juda, and Simon? and are not his sisters here with us? And they were offended at him.

4 But Jesus said unto them, A prophet is not without honour, but in his own country, and among his own kin, and in his own house.

> 5 And he could there do no mighty work, save that he laid his hands upon a few sick folk, and healed them.
> 6 And he marvelled because of their unbelief. And he went round about the villages, teaching.

If unbelief hindered Jesus from ministering effectively (Mark 6:5,6) then unbelief can hinder us from both ministering and receiving healing today. We need to recognize that faith has enemies, and there are hindrances that Satan throws up to stop our receiving from the Word.

We should not be satisfied with doctrine and no experience. We should not rest content when what we read in the Bible is not what we see in our life. We do not want a superficial religion, we want reality.

Today, so many are amazed when they see a miracle. They are amazed when they see an answer to prayer. They are amazed when the supernatural enters into the natural.

Jesus was amazed at their unbelief. He was surprised that the people failed to believe God and take Him at His Word. He was surprised how they failed to receive what God so freely, so willingly, and so earnestly longed to give them. Jesus was amazed when people were not healed.

Doubt And Unbelief

Doubt and unbelief are great enemies of faith. We must seek their remedy. Doubt is a lack of the evidence that builds faith. Faith is based on the knowledge of God's will, so we can see that doubt springs from this lack of knowledge. Hosea cries, "My people are destroyed for lack of knowledge!" (Hosea 4:6).

Doubt exists when we have insufficient evidence to produce faith. When Peter began to sink in the waves of the sea, Jesus lifted him up, saying, "O thou of little faith, wherefore didst thou doubt?" (Matthew 14:31). Doubt is contrasted with little faith, or insufficient faith.

Unbelief is quite different from doubt. Unbelief is willful. Unbelief is disobedience. Unbelief is when we possess the knowledge of God's will, but fail to act upon it. We have heard the Word but we remain unmoved by what we have learned. We assent mentally to its truth, but we give to it no corresponding action. It has no effect upon our lives. We allow it to make no change in our daily affairs.

Paul wrote that those who fell in the wilderness had heard the same message that we have heard, "For unto us was the gospel preached, as well as unto them: but the word preached did not profit them, not being mixed with faith in them that heard it." (Hebrews 4:2). Unbelief has received the testimony of God's Word, but fails to release faith through actions. We are led away by our flesh, by the negative testimony or experience of others. We depend on what we see, are moved by what we feel, and fail to walk according to what we believe.

An Example is Required

The story is told of a man who wanted to help his wife so he took special care to clean the home while she was away. He worked very hard and made a great effort. He cleaned every room. He even washed the dishes and put them away. Everything looked wonderful.

When she returned home, he met her at the door. "What have you been doing," she asked.

"I cleaned the house today" he replied.

She looked at him and said, "I don't believe it!"

Now, she is in doubt. She lacks the evidence to believe what he has said. Nothing from her past gives her any reason to believe this. She doesn't have enough evidence to believe what he has said.

"Then let me show you," he answers, and together they walk through the house. She looks in every room and she is amazed. He didn't miss a thing.

She shakes her head, and says, "I still don't believe it!"

Now, she is in unbelief. She has sufficient evidence to believe it, but refuses what she knows to be the truth!

This comical illustration helps us see the difference between doubt and unbelief. The cure for doubt is time spent reading and listening to the Word of God, for faith comes by hearing the Word of God, (Romans 10:17). Like the woman, we walk around and see what has been done. When the knowledge of God's will is made known, faith is present, and we can be confident and bold to stand upon His promises. We gain sufficient evidence to believe, and we can intelligently cooperate with the Word of God.

But we must make that decision to believe, to be united to the will of God through our faith and by our actions.

While doubt is cured by more of the Word, unbelief must be cured by repentance, and often by prayer and fasting.

The Bible declares that "whatsoever is not of faith is sin," (Romans 14:23). It is necessary to restore our fellowship with God from the presence and effects of unbelief, for unbelief is disobedience to God's Word. It is the willful rejection of the truth. Unbelief is broken by a determined resolve to act on the Word of God in every circumstance and at every opportunity. Unbelief is removed when we gain an understanding of the Word, and learn how to apply it in our lives.

In the face of unbelief, Jesus "went about the villages teaching," (Mark 6:6). He gave instruction in the Word, and through teaching they found understanding. The truth alone sets no one free. It is the "knowledge of the truth" that sets us free, and that knowledge comes when we "continue in the Word" and are His disciples, (John 8:31,32).

Just hearing the Word is not enough, but you must "mix faith" with what you hear, or you must incorporate what you hear into your daily life.

The knowledge of God's will enables us to act intelligently upon the Word of God.

If you cannot apply what you have heard, you have not found the understanding that God desires for you to gain from its principles.

The father of the epileptic boy cried out, "Lord, I believe; help thou mine unbelief," (Mark 9:24).

The man had no doubt. He said he believed. He believed the Scriptures, but he failed to give what he believed the priority over what he could feel or see.

Remember, we are to "walk by faith, and not by sight," (2 Corinthians 5:7).

When we allow what we see and feel to dictate our actions, what we believe in our heart becomes ineffective.

We pray one thing, but say another. We pray for healing, but we speak sickness and disease. Our lives are filled with unbelief.

The man said to Jesus, "help my unbelief." The presence of unbelief was the issue and hindered the man's faith. Unbelief was an enemy to his faith.

Later, the disciples came to Jesus and inquired about their inability to deliver the boy.

> **Matthew 17:19-21**
> 19 Then came the disciples to Jesus apart, and said, Why could not we cast him out?
> 20 And Jesus said unto them, Because of your unbelief: for verily I say unto you, If ye have faith as a grain of mustard seed, ye shall say unto this mountain, Remove hence to yonder place; and it shall remove; and nothing shall be impossible unto you.
> 21 Howbeit this kind goeth not out but by prayer and fasting.

Many have missed in these verses the central truth that Jesus was trying to convey. They assume that prayer and fasting is necessary to cast out certain types of demonic spirits. This is true, but only in a certain context.

First, the name of Jesus is more powerful than any evil spirit, and we have been given "power and authority over all devils," (Luke 9:1).

Second, Jesus has already declared "nothing shall be impossible unto you," (Matthew 17:20).

How can it be said that this kind of evil spirit will not go out "but by prayer and fasting?" Prayer and fasting does not remove the evil spirit. Jesus did not stop to pray and fast before ministering to the boy. He had already spent his time in prayer and fasting. Prayer and fasting had already had their effects upon His spiritual life.

To what does He refer when He says, "This kind goeth not out but by prayer and fasting?" He was referring to the hindrance to the boys deliverance, and to the enemy of their faith. He was referring to their unbelief. This kind of unbelief goes out by prayer and fasting.

Why couldn't we cast the demon out? they asked. Because of your unbelief, was His answer, and unbelief is removed through our prayer and fasting.

13

The Good News

Acts 14:7-10
7 And there they preached the gospel.
8 And there sat a certain man at Lystra, impotent in his feet, being a cripple from his mother's womb, who never had walked:
9 The same heard Paul speak: who stedfastly beholding him, and perceiving that he had faith to be healed,
10 Said with a loud voice, Stand upright on thy feet. And he leaped and walked.

You know the New Testament was written in Greek; not Ukrainian, Russian, or Arabic, or English. The word translated Gospel is from a Greek word that simply means *"good news."* Paul and Silas preached good news.

It's important that you notice this. It's good news, not bad news. Some people are so negative they can take good news and turn it into bad news!

The story is told of two competing shoe companies in England during the 1800's. They each sent a representative to South Africa to investigate the possibility of expanding their business. They each wanted to out perform the other. Travel was slow in those days, and after arriving in Africa the men wrote letters to report what they had discovered. The letters took some time to return to England, but after some months they arrived.

One man reported back, "There are no customers in Africa. No one wears shoes!" The other wrote, "No one wears shoes! Send money. We must build factories now. Everyone is a customer!"

Two men saw the same thing and responded in opposite ways. A person's viewpoint, whether negative or positive, influences everything he sees. Many people read the "good news" with a "bad news" mentality. They read from the Bible, but they have shaded it with their perspective. Their conclusions are wrong because their viewpoint is wrong.

This man heard Paul and Silas preach good news. His life had not seen much good: he was born crippled and had never walked. Remember that when you read the Bible you are reading about real people. Men and women just like you fill the pages of the Bible. These are not stories, they are historical records about real people. This man couldn't walk. He had lived his whole life in that condition.

Many people with financial problems, emotional problems, family problems, and even sickness or disease are so filled with their problem that they don't want to hear good news when it comes. They are so negative that they cannot see the good in anything.

But this man paid attention, and perhaps for the first time he really hears good news. He listens to what Paul is saying and faith enters into his heart. Paul saw this and recognized that the man had faith to be healed.

Where Faith Comes From

Where did this faith come from? How did this man receive faith to be healed?

He heard Paul speak, and Paul was preaching the Gospel.

Romans 10:17
17 So then faith cometh by hearing, and hearing by the word of God.

The Bible tells us only one way to receive faith. Faith comes by hearing the Word of God. It's the only way that faith can come. Some try to pray for more faith, others try to earn faith by their actions or good works. Faith in anyone comes as a result of hearing the word. The integrity of God's spoken Word is the basis of our faith in Him.

What He has said, He will do. What He has promised He will fulfill. "God is not a man, that he should lie; neither the son of man, that he should repent: hath he said, and shall he not do it? or hath he spoken, and shall he not make it good?" (Number 23:19).

Faith enters our heart when we hear the Word of God. The good news (Gospel) of Jesus Christ includes God's promises to us that He made through His Son. Whatever this cripple man heard gave him faith to be healed. This can give us a better idea of what Paul preached.

Would he have received faith to be healed if Paul preached: *miracles have passed away* or, *God doesn't heal today*? Or, would he have received faith if he heard: *sometimes God heals, and sometimes He doesn't*?

These aren't words that build faith. These statements cannot be the good news that Paul was teaching and preaching!

What if Paul taught the doctrine: *God uses sickness and disease to teach His children*? Would that have given a man who had never walked the confidence and faith that healing belonged to him? Would it fill him with the faith that he could rise up and walk?

None of these statements, or any like them, are good news. None of them are the Gospel. Some people try to preach these ideas and pass them off as God's will. But Paul preached none of these things. These words cannot produce a faith that heals, but rather they destroy all confidence that God wants to heal them now.

The man was healed as a result of his having faith to be healed; and he had faith to be healed as a result of hearing Paul preach the Gospel. Healing has not passed away, but in a large part the preaching of the Gospel of healing has passed away.

It's amazing that men preach doubt and unbelief, and then blame God when faith is not produced in the hearts of the people.

Paul recognized that this man had faith to be healed. Faith comes by hearing the Word. The man heard Paul speak, and Paul was preaching the Gospel. If it doesn't produce faith in the one that hears it then it is not the Gospel. It certainly is not good news.

"The gospel is the power of God unto salvation to every one that believes," (Romans 1:17).

All of God's power is in His gospel, in this good news about Jesus Christ.

How Faith Is Applied

Paul perceived that the man had faith to be healed before the man was healed. Did you notice that? The man had faith to be healed but he was still sitting down. He had the faith, but he had not yet received his miracle. Remember this: the presence of faith does not assure a person that he will receive his miracle.

The faith has to be applied. It has to be released. Many people believe the Gospel. They have heard the good news, and their heart is filled with faith, but just like this crippled man they are still sitting with their problem. Faith has to be released, or activated, before the miracle power of God will go into operation.

Do you remember the woman with the issue of blood? (Mark 5:25-34). She heard about Jesus (faith comes by hearing, and hearing by the word of God) and came through the crowd to touch the hem of Jesus' garment. For she said, "If I touch his clothes, I will be healed."

Her faith made her do something! Her faith was released by her actions and by her words. What she said and what she did agreed with what she believed. Many people believe certain things, but their actions point to something else. They say they believe one thing but they do another thing. Their actions contradict what they believe. Their actions and their words nullify their faith. You apply the power of faith by speaking and acting on the Word of God. Through your actions and your words you can release the faith that you have received in your heart.

Faith is abundantly simple when you realize that it is deliberately acting upon the Word of God.

Paul saw that this crippled man had faith to be healed while he was still crippled. Did you ever wonder why Paul said with a loud voice "STAND UP!" Certainly, God is not deaf. Prayers are not more effective just because of their volume. Shouting doesn't gain the attention of God any more than a silent whisper.

Then why did Paul shout at the man with a loud voice if not to motivate the man to act on his faith? Paul spoke to the man to do what he could not do. Paul told the man who had never walked to walk.

I think the man began walking before he had time to remember he was a cripple! The man responded to Paul's command and acted on what he believed in his heart. The healing power of God was received when the man applied his faith, and he was instantly healed.

Faith Is An Act

From the time I was born I suffered from asthma. It's a terrible disease that fills your lungs and restricts your breathing. Often I would have this horrible sensation of drowning. It was so difficult to breathe. I remember spending night after night sleeping sitting up with my back against the wall. It was the only way I could breathe.

I was raised in a Church, but it was a very religious one. It wasn't filled with the truth of God's Word but with the opinions of men and their traditions. Jesus said "the traditions of men make the Word of God of no effect!" (Matthew 15:6). They taught me that it was God's will for me to be sick. They told me that God wanted to teach me humility through this disease. Of course, that gave me a wrong idea about the character of God.

It wasn't until I was sixteen years old that I heard the good news. It fills me with joy to think of it again. Even though I was still sick, it felt like chains had fallen off of my mind. I began to see God according to the Biblical view, and the more I listened to His Word the more faith grew in my heart. I became a student of the Bible and wanted to learn more about God and His will for my life. Every spare moment you would find me in the pages of the Bible or listening to an audio cassette tape of someone preaching a gospel message.

Jesus said, "the words that I speak to you are spirit and life," (John 6:63).

The life of God came into me and faith filled my heart. At that time, I didn't know what I know now. I was making progress, but it was slow. I had no one to sit with me and teach me the things of God. This is one of the reasons I have written this book. For you, perhaps this is the best way I can sit at your side and help you learn from the Bible.

During this time, I was depressed about the asthma

because I wanted to play sports. The sickness made it almost impossible. When I should have been training and exercising I was lying in bed sick.

I remember the day that faith became stronger than doubt, and I acted on what I believed.

I was lying in bed, my lungs filled with fluid. My breathing was heavy, slow and very difficult. During times like this I had to concentrate to read because it was so hard just to breathe. It was easier to put the Bible down, close my eyes and let the sickness dominate me.

But this time there was something on the inside of me that wouldn't lay down and accept defeat. I had fed my spirit from God's Word and it had grown strong. My body was weak, but I was strong on the inside. It was the first time that I realized I had the faith to be healed. In fact, I believed I was healed.

At times before I would think thoughts like this: "I wish I was healed so I could play football…" and sadness would fill my mind. I would lie there so discouraged. I would wonder why God had made me like this and not like other people.

But this time different thoughts filled my mind. I had never thought them before. Inside myself I asked, "What would I be doing today if I was healed?" I realized that I would probably be training to prepare for the new season of sports. "If I was healed, I would put on my shoes and run a mile to develop my body. I wouldn't be lying in bed all day, that's for sure!"

Then I said something out loud with my mouth that shocked me: "Sick people lie in bed all day. I believe I am healed. Healed people don't stay in bed!" I didn't honestly know what I said. I had to listen to myself say it. You see, it didn't come out of my mind it came out of my heart. I had put the Word of God in my heart and it had dominated my mind. Faith was stronger than doubt and faith was beginning to speak.

Remember, faith is not making yourself believe. Faith is when you cannot be made to doubt.

My faith had confronted me and I knew that now it was time to act. I swung my legs out of bed and put my feet on the floor. I had to hold my head in my hands for a few moments and think about what I needed to do. It took everything I had to stand up, get dressed, and put on my shoes to run. I would lean over to tie my shoes, but then have to straighten up again to catch my breath. It felt like every time I bent over to tie my shoes I was diving under water and holding my breath. Finally, I was dressed and ready to go exercise.

In my mind, I felt foolish. My mind was telling me this was crazy. My mind was telling me that I was going to kill myself. I am sure the devil was telling me that, too.

But I was acting on the faith in my heart and not the doubts in my head. I walked through the house to go outside. My father saw me, and surprised at seeing me up, he said, "What are you doing?"

"I'm going for a run," I said, having to stop and catch my breath just to be able to speak out loud. I ignored his questioning look and walked outside.

From our home the road runs up hill. Once my feet touched the road I tried to begin to run. It was more like a shuffle. My body was already desperate for more oxygen. My head was faint and my lungs were burning. I felt a wave of panic sweep over me and I thought I was not going to make it. I began to stumble. My feet were so heavy.

But on the inside I began screaming. Not out loud with my mouth, but on the inside I was screaming, "I believe I am healed!" I stumbled again and nearly fell down, but inside my faith was beginning to stand up.

"I believe I am healed!"

Then the devil spoke to me, and he said, "I'm going to kill you now!" Satan is always afraid when you act on the Word of God. He will fight you to steal your deliverance.

And from the inside of me words began to flow: "You can't kill me, devil. I'm already dead. I am crucified with Christ!"

And then I did a remarkable thing. I was running, or trying to run up a hill. My body was very near to collapse, deprived of oxygen. I was taking large gulps of air, but no oxygen was entering my lungs because of the fluid that filled them. I could hear the sound of wheezing in my ears and echoing through my body. I was drowning and right at the edge of unconsciousness.

At that moment I began to speak out loud. I don't know how I did it. It was impossible, really. I began speaking out loud the verse that was in my heart: "I am crucified with Christ, nevertheless I live. Yet not I, but Christ liveth in me." After every word I had to breathe. I was forcing myself to run and with every step I was speaking out the next word.

I shuffled a few more steps up the hill, trying to run and refusing to stop. I said it again, "I am crucified with Christ, nevertheless I live. Yet not I, but Christ liveth in me."

I began to stagger and almost fell down, so I said it again, trying to shout, "I am crucified with Christ, nevertheless I live. Yet not I, but Christ liveth in me." And I lifted my hands above my heads and said as loud as I could, "Jesus!" then more heavy breathing, and a few steps, "I worship!" another gasp for air, fighting to breathe, "You!"

"Jesus, I worship you!" I was saying as I tried to run, struggling to breathe. I was holding my hands in the air as I ran, praising him.

The next moment I will never forget. I began to say "I am crucified with Christ…" and the power of God came on my body. Instantly, my lungs were clear and free. My breathing was normal. It felt so easy and pure and clean! A strength and a joy filled me that I find hard to describe.

I was healed and I could run.

There was a second miracle that day. Physically, it would have been an achievement to run even one mile. My body was not in good physical condition. I had been without exercise for a long time. But at the end of that first mile I kept on running. With the power of God resting on me I ran eight miles that day.

I have never had asthma again.

14

The Fellowship of Faith

The young man had traveled with me across the nation of Ukraine, and I knew he was watching me every step of the way. He had graduated from Bible School and was eager to enter into his ministry. He was filled with questions, and every moment we could spare he was asking me about this or that spiritual truth. I enjoyed his eager desire to learn. I remembered how I behaved at the same age, and how there was so much I wanted to know.

One evening we sat and talked after the meeting. Our hosts had left us alone for the night. The apartment was quiet. The presence of God filled the room and our fellowship was rich. We both spoke deeply from our hearts and the time passed without notice.

We were surprised when the darkness turned into grey and then brighter into the soft light of a new morning. We had talked of the deep things of God throughout the whole night. He had asked many interesting questions. I remember sharing insights that God had given from His precious Word, and several experiences and testimonies that illustrated their truth. The hours had passed feeling like minutes.

As we were coming to an end, he said to me with excitement in his voice, "You just act like the Word is true!"

"No," I disagreed, "I don't act like the Word is true, I act on the truth of the Word. Faith is made simple when we realize that it is simply acting upon the integrity of God's Word."

"I know God's Word is true!" He said, "But how can you be so bold?"

Many have realized the importance of faith, but like him, faith remains a mystery. Where does faith come from? What if our faith is weak? Can faith grow? How can you act with a fearless confidence? How can you know that you know that you know? These, and many other questions, must be answered.

"You will never be bold until you know God intimately," I said, and then quoting Daniel 11:32, I read "the people that do know their God shall be strong, and do exploits."

It's one thing to know about God, to have facts and information, to learn principles and practices. It's another thing to know Him, to have fellowship with Him on a daily basis and in very intimate ways. Only when you have a personal knowledge of God, and have developed an intimate relationship through the Word and prayer, can you have the boldness to act and do exploits in His name.

"I like to say that fellowship is the mother of faith," I told him. "Faith comes by hearing the Word, but faith grows and becomes stronger by the depth of fellowship that you maintain with your Father, with Jesus, and with the Holy Spirit."

It's living in the presence of God that gives you the calm confidence to step out on the Word boldly, just as Peter stepped out on the water. Many people take much time and discipline to study the principles of the Bible without spending any time with the author.

Knowledge is important, but simple obedience is often more effective because we are walking hand in hand with the Creator of the universe. Never substitute your privilege to fellowship with the Lord by replacing it with the study of the Bible or books in order to gain knowledge. They are two very different practices.

We don't ignore the study of the Bible, but we do it with the aid of the Holy Spirit, as an act of fellowship and communion with the Father. This is how we receive divine life in our hearts on a daily basis. We are feeding our spirits, not our intellects. Our minds may grasp the truth, but our heart grasps the life of God and we are filled to overflowing with the joy of His presence.

Never forget that Jesus said, "The words I speak to you are spirit and life," (John 6:63). The Word of God is alive, and when we partake of the Word we are partaking of divine life.

The Word Of Life

I opened my Bible and shared with him a few Scriptures,

> 1 John 1:1-4
> 1 That which was from the beginning, which we have heard, which we have seen with our eyes, which we have looked upon, and our hands have handled, of the Word of life;
> 2 (For the life was manifested, and we have seen it, and bear witness, and shew unto you that eternal life, which was with the Father, and was manifested unto us;)
> 3 That which we have seen and heard declare we unto you, that ye also may have fellowship with us: and truly our fellowship is with the Father, and with his Son Jesus Christ.
> 4 And these things write we unto you, that your joy may be full.

Notice the key points John is bringing to our attention. First, we recognize that he is talking about Jesus whom he saw, and heard, and touched. He describes Jesus as being the Word of Life. Second, he invites us to have the same level of fellowship with him. And finally, this fellowship with the Father and with the Son will bring us fullness of joy.

How can we have fellowship with Jesus at the same level as John? John clearly said, "that you also may have fellowship with us." We have never had the opportunities nor privileges that John had. We have never seen Jesus with our own eyes, or heard Him with our own ears, or touched Him with our own hands. What must that have been like for John?

John knew Jesus in a very personal way. The Bible even refers to John as "the disciple whom Jesus loved," (John 21:20) obviously referring to a special intimacy. They must have had a wonderful fellowship!

But after the resurrection of Jesus, all those experiences were only memories. A memory of the past is not the same as fellowship in the present. John once had a personal, physical, hands-on relationship with Jesus, but he had to learn a spiritual fellowship. He could no longer hear Jesus with his ears, he could no longer touch Him, or see Him. Now he had to learn to fellowship with the Father, and with Jesus, through the Word of life. He had to learn to walk in communion with the Holy Spirit.

There are two opposite but equally dangerous errors: remembering past failures and remembering past successes. Spiritual nostalgia is a poor substitute for present day fellowship. Your spiritual life cannot remain in the past. We rejoice in what God has done for you in the past, but you cannot live on memories. We need to have a fresh, vital, living relationship with God. We need to seek His face and live in His presence every day of our lives.

Many people will talk about a miracle that God did for them last year, but I wonder what He has spoken to them this morning? We develop a relationship over time, and we spend time with those we love. It's the same with our relationship with God. Knowing God is a pursuit, a life long adventure. As we spend time with Him in prayer, in meditation, in reading the Word, we are partaking of His life. Jesus is the Word of Life, and John encouraged us to have fellowship with this Word of Life.

Remember that faith comes by "hearing the Word of God" not by having heard. What you heard yesterday is not faith for today. Understanding is not faith. Intellect is not faith. Faith is a product of the spirit in living communion with the Word of Life.

The word "life" in the Greek language is *zoe*. It's a unique word and is only used to refer to the life of God. It really describes the life and nature of God as He has it in Himself.

Jesus said, "And this is life *(zoe)* eternal, that they might know thee the only true God, and Jesus Christ, whom thou has sent," (John 17:3).

Our salvation is receiving this eternal life. Jesus came to give us life, and life more abundantly. We have received a new relationship with God that should forever be bearing fruit. John said we would have fullness of joy when we enter into fellowship with God. In other words, the fruit of our fellowship with God is joy.

You cannot spend consistent time with God without it leaving a visible mark upon your life that is easily recognized by others. Anyone who fellowships with the Father, and with Jesus Christ, through the Spirit of God, and by the Word of God, will carry with them through the day the joys of that relationship.

David says, "Thou wilt shew me the path of life: in thy presence is fulness of joy; at thy right hand there are pleasures for evermore," (Psalms 16:11).

The Fellowship of Faith

Spending time with God is our delight. Our times of prayer are times of refreshing, and our time spent reading the Bible are times of enjoyment. It is our privilege and pleasure to be with Him, and to enjoy His presence. "But his delight is in the law of the LORD; and in his law doth he meditate day and night. And he shall be like a tree planted by the rivers of water, that bringeth forth his fruit in his season; his leaf also shall not wither; and whatsoever he doeth shall prosper," (Psalms 1:2,3).

The Apostle John had learned that he could not live in the past. He had seen and heard Jesus, but now he had to maintain a daily fellowship in the presence of a living God. We have been invited to enter into that same fellowship that John experienced. We can have as intimate a communion with the Father as the Apostle John.

Learn the joys of having daily fellowship with the Lord. Spend time each day in His presence. Say to the Holy Spirit "open my eyes that I may behold wondrous things out of thy law," (Psalms 119:18). Approach the Bible with the reality that it is a living book. Jesus is the Word of life. The Word is alive, and everything in your heart and life is "naked and open before His eyes," (Hebrews 4:12,13). The Word searches our hearts, (Psalms 26:2,3). Your spirit is cleansed by the washing of the water of this Word, (Ephesians 5:26). Our whole being is quickened by spending time in its pages, and we are strengthened by meditating on its truths, (Psalms 119:26,28). The Holy Spirit will flood your heart with light when you approach His Word and fellowship with the author of life, (Psalms 119:130). Jeremiah declared, "Thy words were found, and

I did eat them; and thy word was unto me the joy and rejoicing of mine heart," (Jeremiah 15:16).

Meditation is a preoccupation. When you hunger and thirst for the Word of God, when you are filled with longing to spend more time with Him, when everything in you is crying out to have more of God, then you will know and you will be filled with all the fullness of God.

> **Proverbs 2:1-6**
>
> 1 My son, if thou wilt receive my words, and hide my commandments with thee;
>
> 2 So that thou incline thine ear unto wisdom, and apply thine heart to understanding;
>
> 3 Yea, if thou criest after knowledge, and liftest up thy voice for understanding;
>
> 4 If thou seekest her as silver, and searchest for her as for hid treasures;
>
> 5 Then shalt thou understand the fear of the LORD, and find the knowledge of God.
>
> 6 For the LORD giveth wisdom: out of his mouth cometh knowledge and understanding.

This type of great desire begins by simply giving the Word of God the first priority in your life. Let nothing take its place.

Job said, "Neither have I gone back from the commandment of his lips; I have esteemed the words of his mouth more than my necessary food," (Job 23:12). For Job, spending time in the Word of God was a higher priority than eating the daily food necessary to sustain life. It is much more important to sustain spiritual life than physical.

Fasting is when the priority of the spirit excludes the priorities of the flesh.

Whatever circumstance we encounter, whatever trials or difficulties, the first thing that should enter our mind is simply this: What does God's Word have to say about the matter? This is how we make the Word of God first priority in our life.

We learn to abide in Him by living in His presence, and we allow His Word to abide in us by practicing His Word even in the common affairs of daily life.

Secrets Of Abiding In Him

A daily fellowship with God will cut off the occasion to live in sin.

True spiritual life is in Christ alone, and the life He promised to bring abundantly is only received from the vine, moment by moment abiding in Him. Broken fellowship, though not costing one his place in heaven, does cost heaven's place in him.

John 15:1-7

1 I am the true vine, and my Father is the husbandman.

2 Every branch in me that beareth not fruit he taketh away: and every branch that beareth fruit, he purgeth it, that it may bring forth more fruit.

3 Now ye are clean through the word which I have spoken unto you.

4 Abide in me, and I in you. As the branch cannot bear fruit of itself, except it abide in the vine; no more can ye, except ye abide in me.

5 I am the vine, ye are the branches: He that abideth in me, and I in him, the same bringeth forth much fruit: for without me ye can do nothing.

6 If a man abide not in me, he is cast forth as a branch, and is withered; and men gather them, and cast them into the fire, and they are burned.

7 If ye abide in me, and my words abide in you, ye shall ask what ye will, and it shall be done unto you.

George Muller once wisely said, *"It is not possible to live in sin, and at the same time, by communion with God, to draw down from heaven everything one needs for the life that now is..."*

Be quick to restore your fellowship with the Lord, should it ever be broken. "If we confess our sins, he is faithful and just to forgive us our sins, and to cleanse us from all unrighteousness," (1 John 1:9).

Confess your sins to God, acknowledge them before Him, and you will find Him quick to forgive. He is faithful to forgive, meaning He will do it every time. There is no end to God's mercy. As Jeremiah has said, "It is of the LORD'S mercies that we are not consumed, because his compassions fail not. They are new every morning: great is thy faithfulness," (Jeremiah 3:22,23). He is also just to forgive. Every mercy granted you is justice in the eyes of God, for "All we like sheep have gone astray; we have turned every one to his own way; and the LORD hath laid on him the iniquity of us all," (Isaiah 53:6).

Only sin can break your fellowship with the Lord, and the blood of Jesus cleanses us from all sin. You must know that the enslaving power of sin is broken, that the penalty of sins past and present are satisfied, and that victory over sin and its temptation is provided.

When we come before the Lord to abide in Him, and to allow His words to abide in us we place ourselves in a position to receive from the Vine. The Holy Spirit fills us with His living presence. The power of the Holy Spirit to convict is far greater than the power of sin, or the devil, to tempt. We choose to yield to either, and the motives to yield to the Spirit are so much greater than the motives to yield to the flesh.

The very instant you repent of sin you are cleansed from all unrighteousness. You are again abiding in Him. Yield to the Spirit, and live in the abiding presence of the Lord. Surrender your heart, your soul, and your life to pursue this one great passion.

We cannot expect to receive from Heaven unless we are abiding in Him, drawing from the Vine everything that we need in our spiritual life. Jesus made it clear that we would never bear fruit apart from abiding in Him.

Rees Howells, a wonderful man of prayer, was once facing a great financial crisis. His ministry, and many people, would suffer loss unless a miracle was received. He remarked,

"We were in the school of faith, and there is nothing to be compared with having to be delivered to keep you abiding: you will never do it without."

He allowed the pressures and problems of life to drive him deeper still into the presence of God, receiving the life of God from the Vine.

Notice what Jesus emphasized concerning our abiding in Him. This position of abiding is twofold: we abide in Him, and His Word abides in us. In such a relationship, we have been given a tremendous privilege. Our wills become one with Him, united in purpose and intent. We are no longer seeking the will of God as something external, but we have learned to walk and live in the will of God. Our abiding, our unity with Him, is so intimate that what we will about a certain thing is considered the will of God. We are to ask whatever we will in this or that situation, and it is done.

On several occasions, when I have gone before the Father in prayer, about severe problems in my life and ministry, I have been startled at the reply of my King. Several times the Spirit of the Lord has asked me, "What do you want done? What shall I do…" in this or that situation.

God has made it simple for every man to know His will and His Word. Jesus said, "If any man will do his will, he shall know of the doctrine, whether it be of God, or whether I speak of myself," (John 7:17). Notice that our will to obey comes before our knowledge of the doctrine. A doctrine is a teaching of the revealed will of God. Our knowing is dependent on our willingness to obey. We hesitate the matter, as if to make a choice based on preference, when we want to know God's will first. If we delay, wanting to know His will before we choose to obey, then it is not His will at work but our own, seeking our own selfish ambitions.

But when we live in fellowship with Him, we have chosen His will, and through our abiding He reveals His will to us through His Spirit. We become one with His will as we are one with Him.

This reveals the depth of fellowship that God so deeply longs to have with us. Remember, "God is faithful by whom we were called into the fellowship of His Son Jesus Christ our Lord," (1 Corinthians 1:9). God is faithful to reveal all to us, and to impart His will to us as members and part of the Vine.

Abiding in Him, fellowshipping with the Lord, is how God manifests Himself first to us, and then to the world through us. He has chosen to make us His temple, as He has said, "I will dwell in them, and walk in them; and I will be their God, and they shall be my people. Wherefore come out from among them, and be ye separate, saith the Lord, and touch not the unclean thing; and I will receive you, And will be a Father unto you, and ye shall be my sons and daughters, saith the Lord Almighty," (2 Corinthians 6:16-18).

God desires us to live holy, as He is holy, in order to manifest Himself to us in stronger and greater measures. As we abide in Him, become one with Him, fellowship with Him, then we are empowered to walk as He walked. Our faith will grow and flourish, and we will do exploits in His name!

15

The Origin of Sickness and Disease

When we understand the origin of sickness and disease, we prevent a myriad of errors from creeping into our thinking.

Suffering forces us to ask many important questions and they deserve biblical answers. Where does sickness and suffering come from, and why?

It is impossible to read the Psalms and Proverbs without encountering these very questions. Nearly every page reveals, in one way or another, how to live in victory, prosperity, and health; and here we find promises of long life granted to those who walk according to God's wisdom.

Proverbs 3:1,2

1 My son, forget not my law; but let thine heart keep my commandments:

2 For length of days, and long life, and peace, shall they add to thee.

A fair reading of Psalms and Proverbs will quickly illustrate that we are expected to learn from God's laws and commandments, not from suffering, sickness or pain; and that if we obey His commandments we will escape sickness, poverty, suffering and enjoy long life.

There are reasons why good things happen in life, and equally true, there are reasons why bad things happen in life.

Proverbs 26:2

2 As the bird by wandering, as the swallow by flying, so the curse causeless shall not come.

There is a reason, or a cause, when trouble comes. Sometimes it takes moral courage just to face this truth. You may not be personally responsible for everything that happens to you in life, but you are personally responsible for what you do when those things happen to you.

Never forget, **Psalm 34:19:**

19 Many are the afflictions of the righteous: but the Lord delivereth him out of them all.

Our heart goes out to anyone who is suffering, but it should be kept clearly in mind that Jesus never suggested anyone remain in their suffering, nor did He ever suggest there was any lesson to be learned through suffering.

If we walk in the love of God, even as Jesus was moved by compassion, we will always strive to deliver people from their suffering. Sympathy goes down to their level of sickness, pain and suffering, and compassion lifts them up and out.

People enduring pain or tragedy very often try to find a purpose in their suffering. They wrestle with the idea of evil in the great plan of God. "Why did this happen" becomes a more important question than "how can I be healed?" In the experience of their pain they devise philosophical arguments rather than biblical doctrine. They ask, "why did God do this to me?"

There is an endless stream of scholarly books discussing these sensitive topics. Sadly, many of them begin wrong and therefore end worse. They assume God is the ultimate cause of sickness and disease, and Satan (*if he even exists in their mind at all*) is little more than a servant or tool to accomplish God's grand designs.

How do brilliant and educated people arrive at these false conclusions? Having read many such books, I have observed that their faulty conclusions are not due to the arguments of their logic, but rather to the doctrines and principles that they fail to take into account.

Let's briefly consider a few subjects that I find are crucial to understand when discussing this subject and make some general comments here and in the chapters that follow.

The Immutability of God

The Bible clearly states that God is not a respecter of persons and that His character is immutable, or unchanging. The immutablity of God has been a pillar in the Church's doctrine of God throughout history.

Much of the philosophical reasoning which seeks to find purpose in suffering, or a divine plan in the presence of evil, requires a change in God's relational actions toward Man, and a change in God's revealed nature and character.

For example, to believe that miracles have ceased is to believe that God's nature has changed, for it is He "who alone doeth great wonders: for his mercy endureth for ever," (Psalms 136:4).

God performing miracles ("who alone does great wonders") magnifies the character of His mercy by action; one might say because God is merciful, He does great wonders. To diminish either His mercy or His miraculous works would be a degradation of His character, making Him no longer an immutable God. To put it simply, if God can change or is changed, He is no longer God. If God's mercy even once compelled Him to "do great wonders" then He will always do the same given He is always the same.

The Reality of Satan

The Bible clearly states the existence of the person of Satan, the devil.

As C. S. Lewis wrote in his preface to *The Screwtape*

Letters,

> *"There are two equal and opposite errors into which our race can fall about the devils. One is to disbelieve in their existence. The other is to believe, and to feel an excessive and unhealthy interest in them."*

The Bible presents Satan as the enemy and teaches us how to deal with him.

Personal Responsibility and Man's authority

The Bible clearly states that Man has been given a delegated authority with which he is to rule and take dominion over Satan and all his works. No more can we ask the question "Why did God do this to me?" when we understand that God has entrusted His authority into our own hands. One ought to ask, "What am I going to do about this?"

The Devastating Consequences of Sin

The Bible clearly states how sin opens the door to both the devil, and sickness and disease.

While the Scriptures declare that the "wages of sin is death," many sympathetic people troubled by the existence of pain and suffering try to remove sin from the equation entirely. Sin is still working sickness and death in Mankind.

How evil is sin? In short, our view of sin should equal the sum total of all its consequences. Every stroke of evil that befell Man throughout all of history is the sum total of sin's measure. Discussions concerning sickness and disease rarely take that into account.

Remember, if your view of sin is weak, then your view of the grace of God is weaker still.

God Is A Good God

There is a wide gulf between the work of Satan and the work of God. Satan is continual evil and God is continual good. It is important that we understand this simple truth. It affects how we esteem the character of God, and how we value His love and His mercy. It also affects how we stand against, and withstand, the work of Satan and the attack of sickness and disease made against our bodies. We must learn to aggressively resist sickness as much as we resist sin, for their author and perpetrator is the same; and both are contrary to the will of God.

As my dear friend Robert Hawk has said,

"We will never fight something if we just accept it as a part of life... Worry, fear, anxiety, sickness, poverty, unforgiveness and the cares of life will ultimately paralyze us and lull us to sleep until we see those things the way that God sees them. He hates those things because they separate us from the promise that He brings and the freedom and relationship that He has given us and offers us. Stand up and fight against those things..."

James exhorts us, "Do not err, my beloved brethren. Every good gift and every perfect gift is from above, and cometh down from the Father of lights, with whom is no variableness, neither shadow of turning," (James 1:16,17). God is the source of all blessing and good. We never err so far from the truth as when we think God is the cause of our problem, or sickness, or disease.

The Bible keeps it simple so a child can understand it: God is good, and the devil is bad. Don't underestimate its value because it is simple.

Isaiah cried out against those who would attribute evil and calamity to God, "Woe unto them that call evil good, and good evil; that put darkness for light, and light for darkness; that put bitter for sweet, and sweet for bitter!" (Isaiah 5:20).

Whatever you accept as being the will of God immediately becomes unavoidable in your life. How can you resist God? If you believe that sickness and disease comes from His hand, then you are defeated and must submit to its attack upon your life. You will lie down and allow its awful consequences to run their course in your life. You will deprive yourself of blessing, joy and health by your failure to realize this one liberating truth: sickness does not come from God, but the devil, and should be resisted as a work of hell.

These false teachings rob the believer of his inheritance in Christ Jesus. When sickness is seen to be from God, there is no ability to resist, and no basis for faith to be healed. Satan has deceived, and thereby completely defeated, the one who sees sickness to be the will of God.

It is necessary, through the Word of God, to inform such people, "in meekness instructing those that oppose themselves; if God peradventure will give them repentance to the acknowledging of the truth; And that they may recover themselves out of the snare of the devil, who are taken captive by him at his will," (2 Timothy 2:26).

When we look to those who are sick, or diseased, or oppressed, we must change our heart-rending cry of "Why, God?" to a more bold, confident and overcoming statement of faith: "Satan, leave God's children alone!"

Jesus never once tolerated Satan to operate freely nor without resistance. He never once justified failure to receive.

He is not pleased when His children are overthrown by the enemy, (1 Corinthians 10:5). Wherever Satan's works were encountered, He confronted them. Demons were cast out publicly, even in the middle of the synagogues. Religious leaders were confronted boldly whenever their teachings or attitudes opened the door for Satan to operate. Men and women were healed on the Sabbath day, in direct opposition to the religious laws of the day. Satan was given no quarter, no rest, and no tolerance.

Paul commands us to "leave no room for the devil," (Ephesians 4:27).

Satanic Oppression

> **Acts 10:38**
> 38 How God anointed Jesus of Nazareth with the Holy Ghost and with power: who went about doing good, and healing all that were oppressed of the devil; for God was with him.

We understand that everyone Jesus healed was oppressed of the devil. The Greek language here is vivid, and the word translated "oppressed" carries with it the idea *"to exercise harsh control over someone, or to use one's power against someone."* Sickness is the result of Satan using his power over the infirm.

Jesus "healed them that had need of healing" (Luke 9:11) and very often He ministered to the multitudes, so that "all they that had any sick with divers diseases brought them unto him; and he laid his hands on every one of them, and healed them," (Luke 4:40). His fame continued to grow and the word spread that everyone was being healed. People began to gather from many cities and villages. Many came from great distances. We read that "when the men of that place had knowledge of him, they sent out into all that country round about, and brought unto him all that were diseased; And besought him that they might only touch the hem of his garment: and as many as touched were made perfectly whole," (Matthew 14:35,36). Again, note the emphasis that everyone was healed.

A simple reading of the New Testament proves that every sickness and every disease is a work of the devil, and contrary to the will of God. Jesus was anointed with the Holy Spirit and with power to heal all that were oppressed of the devil.

Jesus healed all that had need of healing when they met the conditions of faith that were presented to them. Every healing in the ministry of Jesus was a deliverance from Satan's oppression, and as He healed all that came to him, time after time, we understand that all sickness and all disease is a work of the enemy.

Jesus boldly declared, "The thief (Satan) cometh not, but for to steal, and to kill, and to destroy: I am come that they might have life, and that they might have it more abundantly," (John 10:10).

Satan is the cause of all sickness and disease, and he spreads his evil work through a host of evil spirits that obey him. Our warfare is not with flesh and blood, but we are to stand "against the principalities, against the powers, against the world-rulers of this darkness, against the spiritual hosts of wickedness in the heavenly places," (Ephesians 6:12). This organized host spreads sin and sickness through Satanic strategies. Men are taken captive through their influence and walk "according to the course of this world, according to the prince of the powers of the air, the spirit that now worketh in the sons of disobedience; among whom we also all once lived in the lust of our flesh, doing the desires of the flesh and of the mind, and were by nature children of wrath, even as the rest," (Ephesians 2:2,3).

A Spirit Of Infirmity

Luke 13:11-17

11 And, behold, there was a woman which had a spirit of infirmity eighteen years, and was bowed together, and could in no wise lift up herself.

12 And when Jesus saw her, he called her to him, and said unto her, Woman, thou art loosed from thine infirmity.

13 And he laid his hands on her: and immediately she was made straight, and glorified God.

14 And the ruler of the synagogue answered with indignation, because that Jesus had healed on the sabbath day, and said unto the people, There are

six days in which men ought to work: in them therefore come and be healed, and not on the sabbath day.

15 The Lord then answered him, and said, Thou hypocrite, doth not each one of you on the sabbath loose his ox or his ass from the stall, and lead him away to watering?

16 And ought not this woman, being a daughter of Abraham, whom Satan hath bound, lo, these eighteen years, be loosed from this bond on the sabbath day?

17 And when he had said these things, all his adversaries were ashamed: and all the people rejoiced for all the glorious things that were done by him.

This woman had a spirit of infirmity. It had afflicted her for eighteen years until her whole body was bowed together, or bent double. She was not just bent over, but bent double. The Greek word translated "infirmity" is the most common word for sickness. This woman was afflicted by an evil spirit of sickness and Jesus boldly commanded her to be set free and loosed from this bondage.

It is interesting that Jesus said, "thou art loosed..." (verse 12) and then later repeated the same thought in verse sixteen, "ought not this woman, being a daughter of Abraham, whom Satan hath bound, lo, these eighteen years, be loosed from this bond?"

Satan is clearly marked as the source of sickness and disease.

The Greek word translated "loosed" is *luo*. It carries the meaning of loose, break, unloose, or destroy. The same word is used in 1 John 3:8, "For this purpose the Son of God was manifested, that he might destroy *(luo)* the works of the devil."

Jesus loosed this woman from the bondage of Satan. He destroyed the works of the devil. It was the purpose for which He came. Sickness and disease are here shown to be the work of the enemy, and Jesus came to destroy those works. Satan has come to steal, kill and destroy; but Jesus has come to give abundant life, (John 10:10).

Sin No More

Sin entered the earth through Adam, and by it gained mastery over the entire race. The consequences of sin are many and "the wages of sin are death," (Romans 6:23). All the suffering of every man and woman through time and history has been the direct result of the Fall of Adam.

Through this one man's sin death reigned supreme and the Earth was filled with the curse. The original plan of God to bless and to walk with Man in intimate fellowship was broken. Death began to reign as king over life.

> **Romans 5:12**
> 12 Wherefore, as by one man sin entered into the world, and death by sin; and so death passed upon all men, for that all have sinned.

Death entered the earth through sin, and clearly sickness leads to death. Sickness is defined as a curse, and as such has always been connected with the consequences of sin.

> **Deuteronomy 28:15, 60, 61**
> 15 But it shall come to pass, if thou wilt not hearken unto the voice of the LORD thy God, to observe to do all his commandments and his statutes which I command thee this day; that all these curses shall come upon thee, and overtake thee:
> 60 Moreover he will bring upon thee all the diseases of Egypt, which thou wast afraid of; and they shall cleave unto thee.
> 61 Also every sickness, and every plague, which is not written in the book of this law, them will the LORD bring upon thee, until thou be destroyed.

Every sickness and every disease is described as a curse, the result of sin and disobedience, and not a blessing.

Jesus said, "God sent not his Son into the world to condemn the world; but that the world through him might be saved," (John 3:17). We know that Jesus "gave himself for our sins, that he might deliver us from this present evil world, according to the will of God and our Father," (Galatians 1:4). By forgiving our sins, Jesus has canceled the effects of sin. He has eliminated the consequences, which include sickness and disease, with His own blood.

It is important that we are careful to distinguish the origin of sickness and disease. Sickness is always a direct result of sin. Sometimes it is a result of personal sin, but always it is a result of Adam's sin. Sin is the doorway through which Satan enters.

On occasion sickness is a result of personal sin. David wrote, "Fools because of their transgression, and because of their iniquities, are afflicted," (Psalms 107:17). We have only to repent of our sins, and "He is faithful and just to forgive us our sins, and to cleanse us from all unrighteousness," (1 John 1:9).

Notice when Jesus healed a crippled man and later confronted him in the temple:

> **John 5:14**
> 14 Afterward Jesus findeth him in the temple, and said unto him, Behold, thou art made whole: sin no more, lest a worse thing come unto thee.

Here we see the cause of sickness and disease to be the personal sin of the individual. We cannot expect to walk in Biblical blessings unless we walk in Biblical truth. Often, restoring our fellowship with God is sufficient to allow the healing power of God to flow. Many have been healed while praying a prayer of repentance.

A woman came to me who was in terrible discomfort. Her spine was curving because one of her legs was longer than the other. It placed an improper pressure on her spine, and the pain was growing worse. She wore special shoes with one raised like a platform to relieve the pressure.

We prayed for her, but there was no change. Kneeling, I began to pray for her a second time, and when I laid my hands on her leg the Lord said to me, "Ask her about her neighbor."

I stood up and began to talk to her. I said, "Tell me about your neighbor." She was shocked at my question, and began to share with me about her relationship with her neighbor. It was filled with strife, anger, and even hatred. The situation was a tangled mess. While she spoke, her entire countenance changed. I could tell by the tone of her voice that she was living in unforgiveness.

"You need to repent of unforgiveness," I said. "It's important that you release her from these things, and speak peace to the situation." I instructed her for a few moments on the importance of walking in love towards those who curse us and despitefully use us. I took her by the hand and led her in a prayer for her neighbor. Then she prayed, asking God to forgive her from the sin of unforgiveness. She wept before the Lord as she prayed out of a sincere heart.

After she was done praying, we examined her again. Her leg was completely restored and her back was completely well. God had healed her while she prayed. On still other occasions, we must realize that personal sin may not be involved at all. Children are born sick or deformed. Certainly, we cannot look to their sins as the source of the problem. They are innocent, but still afflicted.

John 9:1-7
1 And as Jesus passed by, he saw a man which was blind from his birth.

> 2 And his disciples asked him, saying, Master, who did sin, this man, or his parents, that he was born blind?
> 3 Jesus answered, Neither hath this man sinned, nor his parents: but that the works of God should be made manifest in him.
> 4 I must work the works of him that sent me, while it is day: the night cometh, when no man can work.
> 5 As long as I am in the world, I am the light of the world.
> 6 When he had thus spoken, he spat on the ground, and made clay of the spittle, and he anointed the eyes of the blind man with the clay,
> 7 And said unto him, Go, wash in the pool of Siloam, (which is by interpretation, Sent.) He went his way therefore, and washed, and came seeing.

Jesus responds to the disciples question with a definite answer. They asked him, "who sinned, this man or his parents?" They made the assumption that the man was born blind due to sin, but could not put their finger on where the sin occurred.

Jesus answered and said, "Neither the man or his parents sinned."

I would like to present an alternative translation of the text by simply moving a punctuation mark. I first saw this suggested in the writings of the great pastor, G. Campbell Morgan, in his commentary on the Gospel of John.

If we are not careful we will make false assumptions that are not consistent with Biblical truth. Many of our modern translations have added their own commentary. They draw conclusions where Jesus was silent. Jesus answered the disciples question directly and added no further comment. They asked was it the fault of the parents or the man himself?

Jesus replied, "Neither." Note the period.

He then proceeds to say, "That the works of God should be made manifest in him, I must work the works of him that sent me."

Many translations incorrectly connect this new thought to the conclusion of Jesus answer. They consider it further elaborating on the disciples' question, and a key to identify the source of the man's blindness. They sometimes add words that do not exist in the original Greek texts. Several add the phrase, "but he was born blind in order…" leading us to believe that the man was born blind by the will of God "that the works of God should be made manifest in him."

This is a contradiction in logic; neither does it hold any credibility in the Greek language. It simply doesn't exist in the original text. More important, such an interpretation is not consistent with other Scriptures concerning the same issues.

First, remember that the Greek language contained no punctuation. There are no periods, or commas in the original texts that make up the Bible as we have it in the original. These grammatical marks, which control the order of thought, are completely controlled at the discretion of the translator. One can as easily mark the end of any sentence at one place as at another. The grammar, the context, and often a comparison of other texts must guide us.

Second, it's important to look at their question specifically. The disciples asked, "Who sinned?" They did not ask, why was the man born blind? They asked, "Who sinned?" Then we have this statement from Jesus: "in order that the works of God should be made manifest…" This makes no sense grammatically or logically as an answer, and it makes no sense Biblically.

Such an idea makes God the author of sickness and the remover of it in the same breath. It infers that God makes sick in order to have the opportunity to heal. This would stand in complete contradiction to what Peter declared, "How God anointed Jesus of Nazareth with the Holy Ghost and with power: who went about doing good, and healing all that were oppressed of the devil; for God was with him," (Acts 10:38).

According to Peter, this man was not born blind by the will of God. Peter said everyone Jesus healed was oppressed of the devil. That would include this man – he was oppressed of the devil, and by healing the man Jesus "manifested the works of him that sent him."

"For this purpose the Son of God was manifested, that he might destroy the works of the devil," (1 John 3:8).

16

The God of All Comfort

2 Corinthians 1:3,4
3 Blessed be God, even the Father of our Lord Jesus Christ, the Father of mercies, and the God of all comfort;
4 Who comforteth us in all our tribulation, that we may be able to comfort them which are in any trouble, by the comfort wherewith we ourselves are comforted of God.

The Bible is filled with common people like you and I — people who have suffered and endured, people as real in life as your next door neighbor. Jesus ministered to many who were born blind or lame. One man was crippled for thirty-eight years, and one woman suffered from an issue of blood for twelve years. Lepers, who suffered terribly in the flesh and as outcasts from society, came to receive

His healing touch. Mothers begged Him to deliver their daughters, and fathers pleaded for their sons. Religious men, and rich men alike, threw away their reputation to seek healing from the Prophet who came from Nazareth.

Always, Jesus was present to heal their diseases and comfort their suffering. It was compassion that moved Him in His great healing ministry, (Matthew 14:14) and the comfort He gave was the removing of their infirmities, the opening of their blind eyes, the restoring of their crippled bodies, the freedom from plague and disease, the end of leprosy, and the opening of deaf ears. He stopped the flow of blood, gave the dead back to grieving mothers, and brought peace to the demon possessed until they were able to sit at His feet in their right mind and hear the wonderful message of God's love.

His heart of compassion has not changed. He lives today to "save them to the uttermost that come unto God by him, seeing he ever liveth to make intercession for them," (Hebrews 7:25). Our risen Savior remains at the right hand of God making intercession for us, and nothing can separate us from His great love, "not tribulation, or distress, or persecution, or famine, or nakedness, or peril, or sword," (Romans 8:34,25). As a result of His never ceasing ministry of prayer, we have become "more than conquerors through him that loves us," (Romans 8:37). He is not distant, nor far removed. In this present-day ministry as High Priest He is easily touched "with the feeling of our infirmities," (Hebrews 4:15).

He is ever present to heal you now, even as you read these words.

What you believe about suffering is important

Many believe that God is a God of comfort, but that His comfort is given to endure the sickness or the disease. In their minds, His comfort does not remove the problem. We find no example of this in the New Testament, especially not in the ministry of Jesus. The purpose of ministry is to deliver the oppressed who cannot deliver themselves.

"Many are the afflictions of the righteous: but the LORD delivereth him out of them all," (Psalms 34:19).

Suffering will either draw a man to God, or drive him away. In many situations men will call on God in desperation; suffering will act as a spiritual catalyst. While in other situations men will perish in suffering, turning bitter against God and shaking their fist in His face while they blame Him for the tragedies of their life.

Some have said, "I thank God for the suffering in my life, for when I was flat on my back in the hospital I looked up to God."

We rejoice that they sought the Lord in the midst of their suffering, but for everyone who sought the Lord there are many others who rejected Him, turned hateful, and left this world without knowing Christ as their Savior.

In my own life, I know it would have been easier for me to have given up, than to have gone on in the ways of the Lord.

Must Christians Suffer?

There is a Godly suffering. Paul taught "that we must through much tribulation enter into the kingdom of God,"

(Acts 14:22). Peter exhorted that "the God of all grace, who hath called us unto his eternal glory by Christ Jesus, after that ye have suffered a while, make you perfect, stablish, strengthen, settle you," (1 Peter 5:10).

There are difficulties that we must go through. God did not deliver the three Hebrew children from the fiery furnace, He kept them in it — but sustained them all the way!

We have the sure promise, "When thou passest through the waters, I will be with thee; and through the rivers, they shall not overflow thee: when thou walkest through the fire, thou shalt not be burned; neither shall the flame kindle upon thee," (Isaiah 43:2).

We do not escape these confrontations. We cannot bypass them. We do not expect to live this life without facing the storms that come to us all. But we do know that He will be with us, and He will strengthen us.

Peter again writes, "Beloved, think it not strange concerning the fiery trial which is to try you, as though some strange thing happened unto you: But rejoice, inasmuch as ye are partakers of Christ's sufferings; that, when his glory shall be revealed, ye may be glad also with exceeding joy," (1 Peter 4:12,13).

Partakers Of Christ's Suffering

But what is Godly suffering? What is our part in Christ's suffering, and how do we glorify God in it?

Are we to suffer the effects of sin? No, for Christ has redeemed us by His blood. He has bought us back with a great price, and there is therefore "now no condemnation to those who are in Christ Jesus," (Romans 8:1). To suffer the penalty of sin when Christ has redeemed us from it is to receive the grace of God in vain. It does not glorify God for us to suffer the effects of sin.

Are we to suffer physically by sickness and disease?

No, for "Christ hath redeemed us from the curse of the law, being made a curse for us: for it is written, Cursed is every one that hangeth on a tree: That the blessing of Abraham might come on the Gentiles through Jesus Christ; that we might receive the promise of the Spirit through faith," (Galatians 3:13,14).

Not one single time does the Bible ascribe God's glory to the suffering of sickness or disease.

Healing Glorifies God

Jesus said, "Said I not unto thee, that, if thou wouldest believe, thou shouldest see the glory of God?" (John 11:40).

Lazarus had died and was buried in the tomb for four days. His death brought no glory to God.

Jesus pointed to the exercise of faith as being the source of Glory that God receives. "If you would believe..."

He raised Lazarus from the dead and many believed on Him as a result, so much so that the chief Priests plotted to kill Lazarus.

Consider these Scriptures where every time we see it is the healing that glorifies God, and not the sickness or disease.

Matthew 9:8
8 But when the multitudes saw it, they marvelled, and glorified God, which had given such power unto men.

Luke 5:25,26
25 And immediately he rose up before them, and took up that whereon he lay, and departed to his own house, glorifying God.
26 And they were all amazed, and they glorified God, and were filled with fear, saying, We have seen strange things to day.

Luke 13:13
13 And he laid his hands on her: and immediately she was made straight, and glorified God.

Luke 17:15
15 And one of them, when he saw that he was healed, turned back, and with a loud voice glorified God.

Luke 18:43
43 And immediately he received his sight, and followed him, glorifying God: and all the people, when they saw it, gave praise unto God.

Godly Suffering

What is Godly suffering? Peter tells us plainly, "Yet if any man suffer as a Christian, let him not be ashamed; but let him glorify God on this behalf," (1 Peter 4:16).

The Bible teaches that Godly suffering involves a choice, and that to abandon one's belief would alleviate the suffering. There is no moral value in suffering without a choice or a decision.

Godly suffering takes place when we refuse to submit to the temptations of sin, and the lusts of the flesh.

> **1 Peter 4:1-3**
> 1 Forasmuch then as Christ hath suffered for us in the flesh, arm yourselves likewise with the same mind: for he that hath suffered in the flesh hath ceased from sin;
> 2 That he no longer should live the rest of his time in the flesh to the lusts of men, but to the will of God.
> 3 For the time past of our life may suffice us to have wrought the will of the Gentiles, when we walked in lasciviousness, lusts, excess of wine, revellings, banquetings, and abominable idolatries.

Godly suffering involves being persecuted for your faith. The three Hebrew children refused to bow the knee to Nebuchadnezzer. They declared that they were ready to suffer the consequences, but they would not compromise their faith in God. The King told them they must burn, and hear their bold reply, "If it be so, our God whom we serve is able to deliver us from the burning fiery furnace, and he will deliver us out of thine hand, O king. But if not, be it known unto thee, O king, that we will not serve thy gods, nor worship the golden image which thou hast set up," (Daniel 3:17,18).

Godly suffering becomes a witness before Kings, and glorifies the true King of Heaven.

Notice how Peter makes a clear difference between Godly suffering, and the wonderful truth that Jesus has provided healing for us through His great sacrifice upon the cross.

1 Peter 2:19-24

19 For this is thankworthy, if a man for conscience toward God endure grief, suffering wrongfully.

20 For what glory is it, if, when ye be buffeted for your faults, ye shall take it patiently? but if, when ye do well, and suffer for it, ye take it patiently, this is acceptable with God.

21 For even hereunto were ye called: because Christ also suffered for us, leaving us an example, that ye should follow his steps:

22 Who did no sin, neither was guile found in his mouth:

23 Who, when he was reviled, reviled not again; when he suffered, he threatened not; but committed himself to him that judgeth righteously:

24 Who his own self bare our sins in his own body on the tree, that we, being dead to sins, should live unto righteousness: by whose stripes ye were healed.

In verse twenty, Peter discusses Godly suffering as "when ye do well, and suffer for it, ye take it patiently, this is acceptable with God."

Notice in verse twenty-four where Peter quotes the Prophet Isaiah, "Surely he hath borne our griefs, and carried our sorrows: yet we did esteem him stricken, smitten of God, and afflicted. But he was wounded for our transgressions, he was bruised for our iniquities: the chastisement of our peace was upon him; and with his stripes we are healed," (Isaiah 53:4,5).

Peter is not telling us to endure sickness and disease, nor to "take it patiently" but rather, he teaches how Jesus bore our sins and carried our diseases. Godly suffering never involves sickness or disease.

Suffering Needlessly

There is no glory in those who suffer needlessly at the hand of the enemy, afflicted with the very sickness and disease from which Christ died to redeem.

Christ redeemed us from the curse of the law. He bore in Himself the penalty and punishment to redeem us from sin, sickness, poverty and death. The Scripture goes into great detail to describe sickness as a curse, including the pestilence, consumption, fever, inflammation, burning rash, hemorrhoids, scabs, madness, blindness, arthritis, boils, and other diseases that could not be healed.

> **Deuteronomy 28:60,61**
> 60 Moreover he will bring upon thee all the diseases of Egypt, which thou wast afraid of; and they shall cleave unto thee.

> 61 Also every sickness, and every plague, which is not written in the book of this law, them will the LORD bring upon thee, until thou be destroyed.

All these things came upon the people "Because they servedst not the LORD thy God with joyfulness, and with gladness of heart, for the abundance of all things," (Deuteronomy 28:27).

We have been redeemed from all these things. Christ became a curse for us, that we might be free from the curse, or we may faithfully say, Christ became a curse for us so that we might be free from all these diseases, from "every sickness, and every plague."

There are two main reasons for these misconceptions about suffering that cause many to suffer needlessly: not understanding the immutable character of God; and not understanding the authority of the believer, and our victory over Satan, the Adversary.

The Immutable Character Of God

In the original creation all was perfection. It was through Adam's sin, and the entrance of Satan, that suffering entered into the earth.

Will there be sickness in heaven? Jesus taught us to pray, "Thy will be done in earth, as it is in heaven," (Matthew 6:10). We cannot accept sickness as being acceptable on Earth, unless we also accept sickness as being acceptable in Heaven.

What you consider to be the character of God is very important. It will have a great impact on your understanding of suffering in this life, of God's will concerning healing, and of your ability to receive the blessings that He has so abundantly promised.

Jesus came to do the will of the Father, (John 5:19, 30; 14:9), and to reveal Him to us. Every time Jesus healed the sick, it was a revelation of the will of the Father.

God's love for His children is greater than our love for our children, and it is the Father heart of God which Jesus emphasizes as a guarantee of answered prayer.

Acts 7:7-11
7 Ask, and it shall be given you; seek, and ye shall find; knock, and it shall be opened unto you:
8 For every one that asketh receiveth; and he that seeketh findeth; and to him that knocketh it shall be opened.
9 Or what man is there of you, whom if his son ask bread, will he give him a stone?
10 Or if he ask a fish, will he give him a serpent?
11 If ye then, being evil, know how to give good gifts unto your children, how much more shall your Father which is in heaven give good things to them that ask him?

He is the God of all comfort, and His Father's heart yearns over you, to heal you and to deliver you.

17

Hear and Be Healed

Have you ever noticed why people came to Jesus? They came with as much intent to hear as to be healed. Luke 5:15 tells us they came to Jesus to "to hear, and to be healed," and Luke 6:17 reads how they came "to hear him, and to be healed of their diseases."

In both cases, the hearing came before the healing.

> **Luke 5:15**
> 15 But so much the more went there a fame abroad of him: and great multitudes came together to hear, and to be healed by him of their infirmities.

> **Luke 6:17-19**
> 17 And he came down with them, and stood in the plain, and the company of his disciples, and a great

multitude of people out of all Judaea and Jerusalem, and from the sea coast of Tyre and Sidon, which came to hear him, and to be healed of their diseases;

18 And they that were vexed with unclean spirits: and they were healed.

19 And the whole multitude sought to touch him: for there went virtue out of him, and healed them all.

How Faith Comes

The importance of hearing is measured by the results, for "faith comes by hearing the Word of God," (Romans 10:17). Because healing is by faith, there will be no healing without hearing first.

The gospels present three aspects to Jesus' ministry: teaching, preaching and healing. Teaching is mentioned twenty-four times, preaching fourteen times. The pulpit is a distinct product of Christianity.

Teaching builds faith and eliminates doubt; preaching excites faith to action; and healing is the manifestation. Teaching affects a man's will by his intellect; preaching affects a man's will by his emotions.

Nicodemus said to Jesus, "we know that thou art a teacher come from God: for no man can do these miracles that thou doest, except God be with him," (John 3:2).

The miracles were a result of Jesus' teaching ministry. Many received a miracle or healing as a result of having first received faith from the message they had heard.

They came to hear and to be healed. Teaching the Word of God, Jesus imparted faith; and once faith was received healing and miracles were the result.

Jesus said in Luke 8:18, "Take heed therefore how ye hear: for whosoever hath, to him shall be given; and whosoever hath not, from him shall be taken even that which he seemeth to have."

And also in Mark 4:24,25 – "Take heed what ye hear: with what measure ye mete, it shall be measured to you: and unto you that hear shall more be given. For he that hath, to him shall be given: and he that hath not, from him shall be taken even that which he hath."

What you hear produces faith, and it may produce faith in the wrong things, if you are listening to the wrong things. When you hear the Gospel, your faith is built on good news. When you hear bad news, your faith is developed in the negative. Fear is faith in reverse. Jesus said, "Take heed how (Luke 8:18) and what (Mark 4:24) you hear."

How You Hear

We take heed "how we hear" by acting on those things that we hear. It is not enough just to listen. We must take action. If we hear the Word of God, and fail to act, we have deceived ourselves.

Be diligent to act upon the things that you hear. As you are reading this book, take the time and consideration necessary to put the principles you have learned into daily practice. "But be ye doers of the word, and not hearers only, deceiving your own selves," (James 1:22).

Matthew 7:24-27
24 Therefore whosoever heareth these sayings of mine, and doeth them, I will liken him unto a wise man, which built his house upon a rock:
25 And the rain descended, and the floods came, and the winds blew, and beat upon that house; and it fell not: for it was founded upon a rock.
26 And every one that heareth these sayings of mine, and doeth them not, shall be likened unto a foolish man, which built his house upon the sand:
27 And the rain descended, and the floods came, and the winds blew, and beat upon that house; and it fell: and great was the fall of it.

Notice the similarities. These two men heard the same message. They had received the same Word. They both were attempting to build a house, which speaks of the affairs of their life. They both went through the storm. As we know, the storms of life come to us all.

Be sure to notice the contrast, or the difference. One man acted on what he heard, while the other failed to act. One man weathered the storm, while the other fell, and "great was the fall of it."

Acting on the Word was what made the difference. One man took heed how he heard, and was careful to put it into practice in his life.

What You Hear

Be diligent to consider what you hear. Do not give time and energy to listen to things that do not contribute to your faith. Don't allow the cares and worries of life to tear you down, but concentrate and focus on those things that build you up and make you strong.

Be as discriminating over what you listen to, what you read, as you are over your diet. You know that a diet of unhealthy food will not produce good health. Why would you assume that listening to negative words, gossip, religious traditions, or evil reports would produce faith?

There are many books that are not worth reading, many sermons that are not worth listening to, and many people that drain your life instead of enriching it. Avoid people who only take from you and drain you of strength and joy. If they come to receive help, that is one thing. If they occupy your time, and constantly drag you down, they should be avoided. Invest your time in people that build you up, or in people who receive your ministry and put into practice the things that you can teach them.

What you hear determines what you believe. Even lies, if repeated often enough, are believed by the very person who tells them.

Taking heed to what you hear also means that you must take heed to whom you follow, or to whom you are listening. We will never find successful results by following unsuccessful people. This is an established principle in the business world, but one sadly lacking in the spiritual arena. As George Mueller has said, "In the supernatural sphere, there is a law of cause and effect."

Faith And Patience

Some years ago, I was invited to address a group of Christian leaders and businessmen in Washington, DC. About twenty people had gathered in a home and after a time of song and prayer, I stood up to preach.

I was tempted to be intimidated by this group of people. They were very successful business people, affluent and influential in the city. I knew their religious backgrounds. The denominations they came from did not believe in divine healing, nor in the present day work of the Holy Spirit. I wasn't even sure how they had come to invite me to speak to them. I didn't want them to reject the Gospel I have been commissioned to preach and I felt very much out of place. It was necessary to constantly remind myself of who I am in Christ, and of what God wanted to do among them. To make matters worse, I had no idea what message I was to share. On occasions the Lord has directed me to approach the pulpit without knowing beforehand what I am to teach or preach. I never enjoy those situations; I am the type of person who likes to be well prepared before I minister. Often, I have 3 or 4 sermons prepared and ready to preach at any one time.

This night I had nothing to say. I had spent the day in prayer, but it seemed as though the more I prayed the more desperate I became. I have come to learn that when the Holy Spirit requires me to depend upon the inspiration of the moment, there are generally great miracles about to take place. As I stood up, trusting the Holy Spirit to guide me, this verse flashed into my mind and my heart:

> **Hebrews 6:12**
> 12 That ye be not slothful, but followers of them who through faith and patience inherit the promises.

I had preached this portion of Scripture for several years. Each time I drew illustrations from the phrase concerning "faith and patience." I would often emphasize the importance of faith and patience in receiving the promises of God. I would instruct believers to make their stand of faith and remain consistent in patience until the answer arrived.

For the first time I saw something I had never seen before. It amazed me and in an instant I was filled with a joy and delight. I saw that this verse isn't emphasizing faith and patience as the subject. It is pointing out who we should follow.

We are not to be slothful, lazy, or apathetic, but we are to be followers. The emphasis is on being a follower and on who we should follow.

I began teaching them along these lines, and asking them questions.

I wonder if you have considered who you are following? It makes all the difference in the world what Church you attend. Many attend a Church which teaches that healing has passed away, or miracles have ceased, and then the people wonder why they live sick and diseased.

If you want to be healed, you will have to stop following those who preach sickness as God's will, or that God uses sickness to teach people, or that the age of miracles has passed. If you want to be healed, you need to follow those who through faith and patience have received healing themselves.

You would never learn to fly an airplane by listening to someone who has never flown. You need to be instructed by a pilot who knows his business. Why would you expect to be healed if you are following someone who doesn't believe in healing?

One time I was driving my car down the street, and I came up behind a large truck. I thought it was stopped at the traffic light, but because of its size I couldn't see the light. I sat there for several minutes. I became restless and annoyed at how long it was taking. *Why wasn't the truck moving*? I asked myself, and after several more minutes I put my car in reverse, backed up, and drove around the truck.

That's when I realized the truck wasn't stopped at a traffic light. The truck was parked! There wasn't even a driver behind the wheel. I had been following a parked vehicle!

I laughed at myself for a few minutes, and then I realized that's how many Christians live their lives. They are following a parked vehicle! It makes all the difference in the world who you are following.

Paul said, "follow those who through faith and patience receive..." Are those you are following actively receiving the promises of God's Word? Are they seeking His Kingdom, diligently seeking Him so as to be rewarded? Are their prayers being answered? Are they hungry for more and more of the of Word, and are they on fire for God?

As I shared these truths with that group of people, I could tell they were getting angry at me. Their faces became very serious. Many of them crossed their arms and stared at me. They didn't agree with the message. It was contrary to many things they believed. I felt like every word I was saying was dropping to the ground and ineffective. Inside, I was crying out to the Lord to help me. I knew that He wanted them to receive far more than I could ever desire.

As I began to think that my message was a failure, and that I was not going to be able to reach them, something happened.

A woman had entered the room earlier with the use of a cane. I had noticed that a man had quickly given up his seat for her as it was more comfortable than others. She sat down gingerly, and remained sitting on the edge of the seat in a stiff and awkward position.

While I was teaching this simple message she became agitated, and started wiggling in the chair. She kept feeling her back with her hand. Her face became flushed. It was drawing the attention of the entire group.

Finally, I stopped teaching and asked, "Sister, what is happening?" Everyone looked at her.

"It's my back," she said. "There is this tremendous heat running up and down my back!"

I asked her, "Has something been wrong with your back?"

"Oh, yes" she exclaimed. "I've not been able to bend for years and I'm in constant pain."

"Sister," I said. "Stand up and bend over." I knew the Lord was healing her. He always confirms His Word with signs following. Wherever the Word is preached, the Lord works with that preached Word and confirms it, (Mark 16:20).

She stood up slowly, and then bent over and touched her toes! She had been completely healed.

Suddenly, everyone in that room wanted to hear everything I had to say! The entire atmosphere changed in an instant. I went on to teach more and more from God's Word, and then prayed for many to be healed and filled with the Holy Spirit. The ministry went on for five hours, and so many lives were changed.

They learned the importance of following those who through faith and patience receive the promises.

Praise Releases Faith

Some years ago, during one of our services a woman entered the auditorium late. I was already preaching, and as she walked in the Lord spoke to me about her. He said, "I want to heal her, today." That encouraged me, and I took notice of where she sat. Because of the distance, I couldn't tell if anything was wrong with her visibly.

When I finished my sermon, I pointed at her and asked her to please stand. I then told her what the Lord had said to me upon her entering. "The Lord wants to heal you today," I said. "Do you need healing?" I had never seen her before in my life.

She nodded her head, and immediately began to make her way to the front. As she approached I could see that she was not walking very steadily. I noticed that she was wearing a wig. She had lost all of her hair.

I spoke to her briefly for a moment at the front of the Church, and then asked her, "What do you need from Jesus?"

She said, "I have a brain tumor, about the size of a walnut," and holding up her hand she showed me the approximate size of the tumor. She said it was located in such a place that the doctors could not operate. They had tried different drugs, but it had not slowed its growth. She had lost all of her hair, and now the increasing pressure from the tumor was impairing her ability to walk. They had taken away her driver's license as a result.

Looking at her, I could see nothing but defeat in her eyes. "The doctors don't expect me to live more than a few months," she said.

Knowing what the Lord had told me, I was very excited; but I quickly recognized that her despair was as large a problem as the tumor itself. She was more established in her problem than in the promises of the Lord. The doctors had given her a sentence of death and all hope was gone.

I laid hands on her and prayed for healing.

Often when I lay hands on the sick, I can sense a tangible power leaving my hands and entering their sick body. The healing anointing can be tangible and perceptible to the touch. Many times it is so strong that the one receiving prayer falls to the floor.

The great missionary to Africa, John G. Lake, once said,

"The tangibility of God's healing power is one of the secrets of ministering healing."

This time I felt nothing. I knew in my heart that she had failed to receive. You realize that God's healing power always comes, whenever we pray, but that sometimes we fail to receive.

My heart went out to this poor woman, and silently I asked the Lord, *what shall I do?*

I knew that if I was not able to help her receive what

God was so eager to give, she would die. I was desperate to show her the heart of the Father, and encourage her to believe His promises.

I opened my Bible and read to her from these verses:

> **Acts 16:22-26**
>
> 22 And the multitude rose up together against them: and the magistrates rent off their clothes, and commanded to beat them.
>
> 23 And when they had laid many stripes upon them, they cast them into prison, charging the jailor to keep them safely:
>
> 24 Who, having received such a charge, thrust them into the inner prison, and made their feet fast in the stocks.
>
> 25 And at midnight Paul and Silas prayed, and sang praises unto God: and the prisoners heard them.
>
> 26 And suddenly there was a great earthquake, so that the foundations of the prison were shaken: and immediately all the doors were opened, and every one's bands were loosed.

"Sister," I asked. "Did you see how Paul and Silas praised God while they were in prison? During this difficult time they prayed and sang praises to God."

She nodded her head.

"Let's lift our hands and thank God for His healing power. Sister, lift your hands and we will all praise God with you." I lifted my hands and began praising the Lord. The congregation joined me, and we all began praising the Lord for healing this woman of the brain tumor.

I noticed that she was still standing there, her hands at her sides, just looking at me.

"Sister!" I said, encouraging her, "Let's praise the Lord together!"

She looked at me and said, "We don't do that in our Church."

I was shocked! "Sister," I said, "this isn't your Church. This is our Church, and this is what we do in our Church! Let's praise the Lord!" I lifted my hands again and with boldness, I said, "Thank you Lord for healing our sister! Thank you for bearing her sicknesses and carrying her diseases on the cross!"

I encouraged her again. Finally, I saw her open her mouth to speak. I leaned in to hear what she was saying. "Praise the Lord," she said quietly, her lips hardly moving.

"That's it, sister!" I said, "Praise the Lord!" I encouraged the people to praise God with us. Many were shouting. "Lift your hands up in the air," I told the woman. "Lift up your hands and praise the Lord."

She looked at me so sadly. "We don't do that in our Church," she said.

I smiled at her, and said again, "Sister, this isn't your Church. This is our Church, and we praise the Lord, and we lift our hands in our Church. It's Scriptural, right from the pages of the Bible. Paul said, 'I want you to pray everywhere, lifting up holy hands…' " (1 Timothy 2:8). I grabbed her wrists and lifted her hands over her head, and looking in her face I kept on praising the Lord.

Very quietly she said, "Praise the Lord." It was hardly

more than a mutter.

With the entire congregation praising the Lord, and now the music playing, I stopped and looked into her eyes. There was such sorrow and fear. My heart nearly broke. Again, I knew that she was not receiving anything from God.

I put her hands down, stood back and looked at her. I looked deep into her soul. "Father," I prayed silently inside. "You have to help me. How can I reach this poor woman. If you don't tell me what to do, Lord, she is going to die."

Immediately, I saw what to do. It's hard to explain. It wasn't a vision. I didn't hear a voice, but on the inside of me, in my spirit, I knew what to do. I am sure joy hit my face as confidence rose up in my heart once again.

"Sister," I asked her suddenly, "Have you seen an x-ray picture of this tumor?"

"Oh, yes," she said. "It's right about here," pointing to the side of her head, "and it's about the size of a walnut." Then she went on to tell me the same story she had told me before. I smiled to myself, amazed at how people are so good at rehearsing evil.

I had to break into her story and interrupt her. "Sister," I said, "What if tomorrow you went back to the Doctors, and had another x-ray taken? Then they show you these two pictures. On the old x-ray you see the tumor, just as you have described it to me; but on the second x-ray you see that the tumor is gone. It's disappeared! Sister, if that happened, what would you do?"

"Oh!" she said, listening to me intently. "What would I do?" Her eyes widened as she imagined it. "I suppose I would scream!" she said.

"That's it, sister!" I shouted. "Scream! I want to hear you scream. When you came in this building, God told me He wanted to heal you today! I've never met you. I didn't even know if you were sick. Look what God has done to show you His desire to heal you today! He's called you out of a crowd of people to get your attention. NOW I WANT YOU TO BELIEVE HE HAS HEALED YOU! I WANT YOU TO BELIEVE THE TUMOR IS GONE! SCREAM, SISTER! SCREAM!"

In a moment of time, in that fleeting second, I could see in her eyes that she saw what I meant. I saw that she had it. Suddenly, she screamed! It shocked us all, and the entire Church began shouting, screaming, and praising the Lord!

"Hallelujah!" I shouted, dancing before the Lord. Faith rose up in her heart and I could see that her actions were not forced or just to please me. She stood there and perhaps for the first time in her life praised the Lord, and she did it screaming!

You know, I'm sure she never did that in her Church!

A week later she came again to our Church. I noticed that her face was beaming with joy. I noticed that during the worship service, she lifted her hands and worshipped God with us.

We all wept for joy when she stood and shared her testimony with us. She had returned to the Doctors. They had taken another x-ray. She examined the first and saw the tumor that was trying to steal her life. Then they showed her the new x-ray, and it was gone! It had disappeared!

It happened just as the Lord showed me.

Jesus Christ is alive! The healing power of God removed that tumor from her body when she released her faith by praising him without shame, screaming His praises!

We do that in our Church and you can, too.

Receive His healing power right now, in Jesus name!

What Must I do to be Saved?

We read in the Bible that when the Apostle Paul was imprisoned and put in chains for his faith, the jailor asked him, "What must I do to be saved?" to which Paul boldly replied, "Believe on the Lord Jesus Christ and you will be saved," (Acts 16:30,31).

I encourage you to pray this prayer out loud right now!

"Heavenly Father, I come to you in the Name of Jesus. Your Word says, "Whosoever shall call on the name of the Lord shall be saved" (Acts 2:21). I am calling on you, Lord. I ask Jesus to come into my heart and be the Lord over my life according to Romans 10:9,10. "If thou shalt confess with thy mouth the Lord Jesus, and shalt believe in thine heart that God hath raised him from the dead, thou shalt be saved. For with the heart man believeth unto righteousness; and with the mouth confession is made unto salvation." I do that now. I confess Jesus is my Lord, and I believe in my heart that God raised Him from the dead. *Jesus is Alive and He is my Lord!*" Amen.

Dale Armstrong is the director of the Armada Network.

If you need prayer for your life, or for more information, additional teaching materials, or to schedule ministry engagements, we invite you to visit us at:

www.armadanetwork.org

or write us at: director@armadanetwork.org